Princess Diana
the Lamb to the Slaughter

Princess Diana the Lamb to the Slaughter

Joy Jones Daymon

Writers Club Press
San Jose New York Lincoln Shanghai

Princess Diana
the Lamb to the Slaughter

All Rights Reserved © 2002 by Joy J Daymon

No part of this book may be reproduced or transmitted in any form or by any means, graphic, electronic, or mechanical, including photocopying, recording, taping, or by any information storage retrieval system, without the permission in writing from the publisher.

Writers Club Press
an imprint of iUniverse, Inc.

For information address:
iUniverse, Inc.
5220 S. 16th St., Suite 200
Lincoln, NE 68512
www.iuniverse.com

Cover design
Michael L. Daymon
Daymon AdDesign

ISBN: 0-595-24362-2

Printed in the United States of America

For Her Royal Highness, Diana, Princess of Wales

"...I was very, very calm, deathly calm. I felt I was a lamb to the slaughter. I knew it and couldn't do anything about it."...
—Diana

Contents

PREFACE xiii
PROLOGUE 1
Chapter 1   WEDDING OF THE CENTURY............ 3
Chapter 2   THE LADY DIANA SPENCER 15
Chapter 3   CHARLES, PRINCE OF WALES 27
Chapter 4   QUEEN ELIZABETH, THE QUEEN MOTHER 37
Chapter 5   THE ROYAL MARRIAGE 47
Chapter 6   END OF THE FAIRY TALE.............. 65
Chapter 7   DEATH OF A PRINCESS................ 81
Chapter 8   UNANSWERED QUESTIONS 91
Appendix A CAST OF CHARACTERS................. 119
Appendix B FOOD IN WARTIME ENGLAND 121
Appendix C NOTES 127
Appendix D BIBLIOGRAPHY...................... 141

ACKNOWLEDGEMENTS

I am indebted to a number of people, without whose help I could not have produced this book.

To my friend, Debra Mock, who is always there for me. My son, Jim, who patiently endured my obsession with Diana, and my grief following her death. My son, Michael, who believed I could write this book and never let me stop believing. To Michael, also, my deepest gratitude for the cover design.

To Valerie Craig for her invaluable technical assistance. To Rifka Kielson, with iUniverse, who patiently answered my unending questions.

To my support group (who, in effect, became my editors): Mike Daymon, Sam Ogden, Elizabeth Erzen, Martha Lancaster, who constantly encouraged me, even as they forced me to reach higher.

I remember my friend now gone, whose whispered "You can do it" I still sometimes hear.

Finally, I am indebted to the army of journalists and photographers, even—perhaps, especially—those whose information was inaccurate or biased. Without them I would never have known Diana, or any of the royal family, nor felt compelled to write this book.

Any errors, technical or otherwise, are mine and mine alone. I have made every effort to be as accurate as possible. I regret any errors.

PREFACE

Why did I write this book—I who never spoke to Diana, who never curtsied to the Queen, who never attended a garden party? The answer is easy. I had to. I had to write it. Diana haunts me and I could see that I would have no peace until it was written.

Still, why me? What did any of this have to do with me? I am still struggling with that question, but I suspect it began a very long time ago.

I was a child of the Great Depression. We were desperately poor. We never actually went hungry, but we struggled for money for necessities. All the people I knew were poor. Many felt hopeless, defeated, but almost everyone could scrounge up ten cents for the "picture show" on Saturday night at the Star Theater. (If you had a quarter you could go to the Ritz.) Many kids spent their entire Saturday afternoon watching cowboys, cartoons, and whatever else was available. This was our escape from a dull and dreary world. At the "picture show" we could vicariously experience the glamour and excitement of the people played by the likes of Clark Gable, Carole Lombard, and Katherine Hepburn. In the darkened theater, sitting in the plush seats, surrounded by the exotic aroma of pop corn and coconut oil, it was easy to forget all our problems for just a little while. The late country singer Marty Robbins told of spending entire Saturdays watching cowboy movies. He said he was never afraid going home across the dark desert because by then he *was* Gene Autry. In addition to the movie—the "entrée"—there were cartoons, "shorts," slapstick comedy, previews of the next week's movies—and newsreels, the 'thirties version of CNN. More and more I was drawn to the newsreels. They were about real people, real events. Already war was building up in Europe. Often there would be shots of King George V and Queen Mary. I thought she was the very epitome of *regal*. She was my idea of what a queen should be just as Franklin Roosevelt was my idea of what a president should be. She remained regal long after she was widowed. She died in 1953 at the age of 86, shortly before the coronation of the Queen. She loved jewelry, adding quite a number of very important pieces to the Queen's jewelry, and she wore it well. Young as I was I realized that Hollywood stars come and go; royalty is forever. I was hooked.

Young and innocent, I thought it incredibly romantic when King Edward VIII (later Duke of Windsor) gave up the throne because he would be unable to "discharge my duties as King as I would wish to do without the help and support of the woman I love." I had no idea of the seriousness of the situation and the constitutional problems involved. In the 'forties King George VI and his consort, Queen Elizabeth (later the Queen Mother), were often seen inspecting the terrible bomb damage in London. The Princesses were almost prisoners in nearby Windsor Castle, for their safety. They would have been safer in Canada, but their mother was not willing to be so far away from them. As she put it: "They won't go without me. I won't go without the King, and he won't go." That pretty well ended the discussion. They were a wonderful inspiration during this difficult time and an unbreakable bond was forged between the royal family and this generation.

I grieved for Princess Margaret when she had to give up Group Captain Peter Townsend, the man she loved, but rejoiced in the wonderful wedding of the Queen to the handsome Prince Philip of Greece.

The Queen and I married the same year—she in Westminster Abbey before the crowned heads of Europe; I in a Methodist parsonage with the pastor's wife and a friend as witnesses. The following year we each gave birth to our first child, a son. For each of us there were two more boys and a girl.

Life was full of minutia and I thought less about the royal family, although I continued to read any magazine article or book that crossed my path. Then there was news that Prince Charles had finally found his bride. I always had a soft spot in my heart for Prince Charles. He always seemed a little sad and lonely to me, always wanting, like any child, his parents' approval and never quite getting it. So I was delighted that he was going to have this lovely girl as a life companion. I watched every minute of the wedding. I kept up with the news of Diana's first pregnancy and rejoiced at the news of the birth of a healthy son, an heir to the throne of England. What wouldn't Henry VIII have given for such a child! I studied every picture. Something was bothering me. Finally I had a chance to really visit England. It was an amazing experience to actually see and visit places I had only read about in history books and novels. When I was growing up the word "American" was never hyphenated as it is today. If it had been I would have been "British-American." Our Congress was modeled on the British parliament; our laws based on British laws; my religion is based on the teachings of an Anglican Priest named John Wesley, so in a sense, I felt I had come home. I toured Kensington Palace, walked in the gardens, gazed at the fairy-tale wedding dress (more beautiful than pictures can show), saw the equally beautiful jewel encrusted satin slippers that I had not seen before. They didn't show in the photos. I looked at the fabulous Crown Jewels—gems so large they don't look real. I saw the Tower of London where Anne Boleyn was beheaded and Princess Elizabeth Tudor was imprisoned. I walked in Windsor Castle and Buckingham Palace. In historic St. Paul's Cathedral I sat where a wedding guest had sat. I came home and studied the pictures some more. Something didn't fit.

Then came Andrew Morton's book *Her True Story*. Even though we later learned that Diana herself had furnished much of the information, I understood that the story was true from Diana's point of view—and that there are always two sides to every story—so I continued to obsess. I heard Charles's interview; I heard Diana's interview—and, later, Andrew Morton's and Michael Tomlinson's, and the Queen's reluctant speech.

When news of her death came, I was in shock like everyone else. Gradually, however, I came to feel there had been a reason for all my searching and obsessing. There were plenty of stories about her—about her clothes and sense of style; about her charm and charisma; about her compassion for the ill, the needy, the elderly; about her "problems." But there was really no story about how she, in sixteen short years, changed the British Monarchy irrevocably; how she changed British history. At various times in history the people have demanded more power (leaving less for the monarch). This was one of those times. Diana's death—and the people's reaction to it—changed forever the perception and role of the British Monarchy. It did require her death. In spite of her sparkling style and fashion, there was a vulnerability about Diana, a sense of fear of failure, fear of abandonment, fear of loss of love, that so many of us around the world felt and responded to without quite knowing to what we responded. I think that is why so many "who never knew her felt that they knew her." And so I felt compelled to write the story of how a teen-aged aristocratic English girl was sacrificed for the British Monarchy. Perhaps there are satisfactory answers to all my unanswered questions. I have not found them. My resources are limited, but my questions are real. This is the story of the Queen England never had—Princess Diana, the Lamb to the Slaughter.

PROLOGUE

"My God! What's happening?" It was the Princess's last words in this life. She felt something cold and hard pressing over her mouth and nose. "I can't breathe—I can't breathe!" she screamed, but no sound came. She strained against it, but she was getting weaker and weaker—and then—blessed oblivion.

He felt her go limp and allowed himself a fleeting moment of satisfaction. He must be very careful. He was carefully looking only at Diana, but he was painfully aware of the barrage of flashbulbs going off continuously. He knew every move, every expression was being recorded. Somehow he must make sure all this film was confiscated. He felt sure he had not made a false move—everything had gone exactly as planned. Still, the photos were an unknown factor and must be destroyed. They were using the plan prepared in 1992 to wipe out Yugoslav leader Slobodan Milosevic, but obviously it had to be modified to fit the present circumstances—and it was essential that every detail be carefully worked out. Something as simple as adjusting the seatbelts so they would come unfastened under stress could not be overlooked. This was the most important operation since World War II, and probably his last chance to show how valuable he was. Paris was the perfect place to put the plan in action. The de L'Alma Tunnel was ideal—even better than most tunnels because of the heavy concrete pillars, and with the couple going back and forth between the Ritz Hotel and Dodi's apartment, the paparazzi were in a frenzy. That made it much simpler to get their agents in and out. Most important of all, in France the accepted medical emergency procedure was to bring the ER to the patient, rather than the "scoop and run" method of the United States and England. It was, of course, imperative that the Princess *not* survive the accident. Many hours had gone into planning an execution that would be, *must* be, seen by the whole world as an accident caused by a drunk driver. (Getting the alcohol into Paul had been the easy part.) First the Fiat and a motorbike forced the Mercedes toward the concrete pillars. The strobe flash gun (designed to disorient helicopter pilots or terrorists) used to blind Paul worked perfectly. The faulty brakes and warning light did the rest—and the air bags. Knowing there would likely be an investigation, there was a well-documented story on file of the car having been stolen and tampered with.

He would have to prepare a statement for the press that would explain both his presence and his departure. It was unfortunate that Trevor Rees-Jones survived, but that would have to be taken care of later (and he might yet die without regaining consciousness). There was no way to be sure how much he saw and understood. With so much happening at once he could very well have believed it was simply an accident. In any event, he would not be talking any time soon. It was too bad Paul had to be sacrificed. He was a good agent, but lately he was getting careless, and anyway—business is business. Sirens and flashing lights announced the arrival of the ambulance. He backed carefully out of the car. Avoiding the still buzzing paparazzi he made quick eye contact with the ambulance crew—all good agents. The Princess was quiet. If she showed signs of reviving they would know what to do. He quietly got in his car, nodded to his companion and they drove away. In his rear view mirror he could see them beginning CPR. Quick and cursory as his examination had necessarily been, he knew she was bleeding internally. They were doing their job—pumping her life away…it was for the good of England.

Could it have happened like this? Will we ever know, or will there forever be questions?

1

WEDDING OF THE CENTURY

The King's patience is growing thin. Year after year he has seen a male child miscarried or stillborn. Finally, risking the enmity of the powerful Spanish King and bringing eternal damnation on his own soul he breaks away from the Pope, proclaims himself Head of the Church of England and annuls his marriage to the aging Spanish Princess, Katherine of Aragon. Now he can marry the young and bewitching Anne Boleyn. Henry VIII understands that, at whatever cost, he must provide an heir for the throne of England. It is for the good of England. It must be.

The magnificent gates of the Althorp Estate clanged shut behind the flower-bedecked hearse that carried Diana's body to its final resting place. Clanged shut, leaving all the rest of us outside, lost, unable to comprehend this unprecedented week. Not a state funeral, but a royal funeral nonetheless. How could that be? For that matter, how could she, so full of life, be dead? Her magnificent spectacular funeral was over. The era of Diana had ended. The reign of Diana, Queen of Hearts was over—and we were not ready.

So why is her face still on so many magazines? Why are books about her grabbed fresh off the press? How can the tabloids continue their weekly saga of Diana?

Who was this woman who made such an impact on the world and especially on the British Monarchy in just sixteen short years? How could she, single-handedly, bring about so much change in royalty? How could she so much affect ordinary people who never even met her? What was it about her that appealed to such a wide diverse population? Who was this woman to whom even the Queen of England bowed?

She was still a teenager, not yet twenty years old, when she accepted the proposal of marriage to the future King of England. It was the century of democracy and monarchies were dropping like flies. The British monarchy—the most stable of them all (its roots stretch back at least a thousand years)—even staggered and tottered from time to time. It was especially weak in 1981 with serious recession resulting in civil riots and loud complaints about the cost of royalty. Yet the royal wedding seemed to be a fairy tale come true and was a welcome diversion. The Lady Diana Spencer was a vision of loveliness in a billowing creation of pure silk ivory taffeta with its twenty-five foot train as she walked down the endless red-carpeted aisle of historic St. Paul's Cathedral in London on the arm of her father. The Prince of Wales, handsome in the full dress uniform of a Commander in the Royal Navy, was heir to the throne of England. Among the wedding guests were heads of state of most of the nations of the world. The event was carefully staged and, in addition to the thousands who lined the London streets, was viewed via television by 750 million people. It was televised to every continent, presented in 34 different languages and captioned for the deaf. Television coverage of the event continued non-stop for seven and a half hours. In the United States more television time was devoted to coverage of the royal wedding than had been for the space shuttle flight or the return of the American hostages from Iran.

Both bride and groom were careful to follow important traditions. The bride's "something new" was her lovely dress, designed by David and Elizabeth Emanuel and fashioned of forty yards of ivory English silk taffeta, embellished with lavish ruffles, lace, mother-of-pearl sequins and tiny pearls, and festooned with billows of fine hand-embroidered silk tulle. The something old was the antique lace that had belonged to Queen Mary (Charles's great-grandmother) appliquéd on the bodice of the dress.

Something borrowed was the Spencer family tiara and her mother's beautiful ornate pearl and diamond earrings. Something blue was a tiny bow hidden inside her gown. Reportedly, her mother added a tiny gold horseshoe for good measure. The wedding band the groom placed on her hand was a thin gold band made from a nugget of Welsh gold from which wedding rings had also been made for Queen Elizabeth, the Queen mother; for Queen Elizabeth II; and for Princess Margaret and Princess Anne. In her bridal bouquet were sprigs of myrtle that were descendants of sprigs from Queen Victoria's bridal bouquet (along with Mountbatten roses in memory of the groom's beloved great-uncle, white orchids, lilies of the valley, freesias—Diana's favorite—and stephanotis). The groom formally asked the bride's father for her hand in marriage. (He was required to obtain permission from his mother, the Sovereign.)

The wedding breakfast for 118 close friends and family members was held in Buckingham Palace and served on gold plate. Three days were required to set up for the wedding breakfast, including the polishing of the gold plate and silver ornaments, placing the snowy white linen cloths and floral arrangements exactly in place and meticulously arranging each place setting. The four-tiered wedding cake, created by Frank Weinholt, weighed over 200 pounds, took six weeks to make and was in itself a work of art. (According to other sources it was created by Royal Navy cooks and required three months to make. Undoubtedly there were a number of wedding cakes, as there had been for previous royal weddings.)[1] Thousands of wedding souvenirs, ranging from magnificent sterling silver items by Garrard, the Crown Jewellers, to commemorative plates, mugs and tea towels were sold. Commemorative stamps were issued by over seventy countries. No detail was overlooked. Covered carriages were on standby in case of rain. The pomp and panoply reminded the world of the power and pageantry that is pure British.

The couple received more than 10,000 wedding gifts, including (for the bride) an antique diamond and pearl drop tiara from her mother-in-law, the Queen, which had been inherited by the Queen from her grandmother, Queen Mary;[2] a diamond and sapphire parure from the Saudi Arabian royal family valued at approximately a million dollars; ornate diamond and pearl earrings from the Emir of Qatar; from the Queen Mother a magnificent sapphire brooch which Diana later had set in an eight strand pearl choker (it became one of her favorite pieces), pearl drop earrings from Collingswood Jewellers; a strand of perfectly matched pearls with a diamond clasp—the list goes on. The gifts actually began with the engagement ring from Charles (his first gift of jewelry), a sixteen-carat oval sapphire surrounded by fourteen diamonds set in white gold. This was followed by other gifts of jewelry, including some from the royal coffers. (From the Queen, also, came a dainty diamond watch, Queen Mary's art deco diamond and emerald choker and other antique pieces). Charles's wedding gift to Diana was emerald earrings and bracelet to match the art deco choker. The honeymoon was a cruise on the luxurious yacht *Britannia*, followed by several weeks at the Scottish royal residence of Balmoral. Within a year the lovely young bride had presented her husband with a healthy son and the United Kingdom with an heir. Everywhere they went crowds thronged and cheered and they were treated as the royals, which they truly were—Cinderella and her Prince Charming—and the whole world basked in the reflected glory. Early pictures of the Prince and Princess show a loving couple, an affectionate husband solicitously assisting his pregnant wife down the aircraft steps (or squeezing her backside at polo!), an adoring wife looking trustingly at her husband for support and guidance, a proud father bringing his newborn son out of the hospital. Pictures of the happy family standing on the deck of the *Britannia* following their first visit to Italy show the couple side by side with Diana holding the baby and Charles supporting Prince William; or the Prince and Princess taking the children to nursery school, or all four riding bicycles on country lanes. Formal and informal family pictures show a happy, healthy family—exactly what the public and the media wanted.

Yet all too soon rumors began to surface—rumors of arguments, days spent apart—rumors consistently denied, either officially by the Palace or unofficially by "reported" comments by the Princess. ("My marriage is just fine, thank you very much.")

Still the rumors persisted. When the Princess left the royal family in Balmoral less than two months after the wedding and returned to London, it was widely reported that she was "bored" with life at Balmoral and was on a shopping binge. In fact, she was seeking professional help for her stress and depression. Like everyone else she had assumed that once the wedding was over she would slip back into relative obscurity, at least until Charles became King. She had not yet admitted that she was bulimic; indeed she did not even know there was a name for her malady. She only knew that she was miserable. Actually, she and Charles had spent many happy hours at the Queen's Scottish retreat, walking, talking, fishing, reading together. There were other times of intense doubt, jealousy, arguing, especially over the role of Camilla Parker-Bowles, but Diana was "besotted" with Charles and he seemed to be in love with her—"whatever in love means." (It is not true that he never loved her. Even if Camilla was his "real love," there is no mistaking the affection and infatuation openly expressed in the early photos. But perhaps not until he was notified of her death did he realize this.) Soon Diana was pregnant and this new development brought about new hope and new concerns. Unfortunately, Diana suffered terribly from morning sickness. Stress plus the bulimia undoubtedly contributed to this. Photos of her during this period show a pale, thin, exhausted princess. One especially poignant photo shows her in a beautiful designer ball gown, perfect make-up, sparkling hair style topped with a diamond tiara. She is sitting erect in her royal chair, hands in her lap as she has been trained. She is asleep.

Bulimia nervosa is a serious, sometimes fatal, eating disorder which affects an estimated two per cent Americans, mostly young women.

The figures are similar for England. Only in recent years has it been officially recognized as an illness separate from anorexia nervosa. There are similarities. Both are eating disorders. Both are related to poor self-esteem, combined with unusually high self-expectations, typically from dysfunctional families. Anorexia is a disease in which the patient believes herself to be "fat"—even when dangerously thin—and continues to diet or even fast until, in some cases, she literally starves herself to death. In less drastic situations there is still malnutrition and all the associated problems. Anorexia is usually experienced by young women who, for various reasons, fear growing up, becoming adults, and subconsciously attempt to maintain their child-like, pre-pubertal bodies. Anorexia, at least in its advanced stages, is quite obvious to the observer. Bulimia, on the other hand, is much more subtle and sophisticated. With bulimia it is possible to "hide" the symptoms. It is characterized by periods of bingeing followed by purging (usually by vomiting or use of laxatives) or by fasting. The bingeing, usually for comfort or self-nurturing, but sometimes just to relieve stress, is followed by feelings of guilt, worthlessness, self-hate, loss of power, even thoughts of suicide, which can only be relieved by "getting rid of" the gorged food.[3] This purging provides such relief, such a sense of being in control, that it quickly becomes addictive. It can go undetected for a long time if the patient is careful because there usually is no drastic weight loss. (Diana did suffer a drastic weight loss but, since she was seen to have a healthy appetite, it was blamed on the stress of the wedding preparations.) This loss of vital nutrients causes severe mood swings; loss of hair and other problems; the excess acid can damage tooth enamel. Bulimia patients tend to always appear happy, fearful of displaying or even acknowledging the underlying rage or misery. They are "the good little girls," the helpers, the neat ones, the peacekeepers.

Diana continued to work throughout her pregnancy, ignoring her indispositions as best she could. She worked throughout both pregnancies—and, while some might think that wearing glamorous clothes and being presented with bouquets might not be hard work, it is when everything has to be perfect, on schedule, and you are constantly being guarded, guided, photographed and criticized. An ill chosen phrase might insult a nation. She could never really relax. As she reached the limits of her endurance (no other queen-in-waiting has ever been expected to do so much) her doctor ordered a "complete rest," so she and Charles flew to the Scilly Isles for rest and relaxation. Immediately there were photos of the couple on a "walk-about" on their arrival. The second day they visited the island of Tresco (more photographers) and the third day they attended a luncheon. Strange way to rest. During this period there is much evidence of a close, affectionate relationship. Still the rumors of terrible arguments ("really terrible rows") continued. The press was unrelenting. The public appetite for pictures was insatiable. We commoners needed to believe that somewhere "happily ever after" really existed. As a result, the rest of us were able to keep up with the progress of the pregnancy on an almost daily basis, but the Princess, in her efforts to be a good wife and a good princess, was using up all her resources.

In the next two years the Princess would accompany Charles on several major tours, including Australia and Canada, and give birth to another son. Everybody loved her. That these tours were planned so early in the marriage gives evidence that the Palace was well pleased with the Princess's performance and felt that she could handle such an assignment. (Actually, she is not Princess Diana. Only if she were royal by birth would she be. She is either Princess Charles—which nobody was willing to accept—or she is Her Royal Highness, Diana, Princess of Wales. However, the public refers to her as Princess Diana or even Princess Di.) During this time Diana trusted Charles to guide her through the protocol and ceremonies (and she always had a lady-in-waiting close at hand). He, in turn, was proud and supportive—at least in public. But day after day of hearing groans on his side of the street and cheers on her side took their toll. Charles was beginning to feel like "the man who accompanied Jacqueline Kennedy to Paris," and found himself apologizing for "not having enough wives to go around." *He* was supposed to be the star. By the time the couple made their first visit to Italy the strain was beginning to show. Diana, unfortunately, read all the press releases and took them to heart. Having been accused of being a "shopoholic," she tried to economize by redesigning some of her outfits and wearing some old favorites. The Italians were not pleased. They saw this as an indication that she did not think they were as important as others she had visited. (The Queen, frugal in so many ways, never wears the same dress twice in public.)

By 1985, to off-set rumors and the more negative press, the couple agreed to do a television interview conducted by Sir Alistair Burnet. The program portrayed doting parents and lively youngsters. The questions and answers were not memorable, except for possibly one. Asked about the wedding, Diana said, "It was terrifying...No, I'm only teasing...Am I?" (It was Charles, during the official engagement interview, who proclaimed his love for Diana, adding, "Whatever in love means."[4] Still, the stories continued. Diana and Charles spent thirty days apart. He was in Scotland while she remained in London. Diana was suffering from anorexia. (These were the stories.) The quarrels and arguments were becoming more virulent. Staff turnover was high (and Diana was blamed for this). In her frustration she told royal reporter James Whitaker, "I just don't sack people!" She probably was responsible to some extent. She felt the people around Charles were sycophants and that was really not good for him. She also knew that many of them had known of Charles's involvement with Camilla and had deliberately kept it from her—or tried to. She would naturally have been uncomfortable with these people. There was something else, something that never gets mentioned. It is customary for the royals to employ homosexuals, for the very practical reason that they do not have families and are more easily able to work the long and varied hours. At this stage in her life, Diana might have felt this to be a bad influence on her boys. She later had very good friends who were homosexuals.

Charles began to complain that when he tried to do or say something serious, what Diana was wearing overshadowed the event. (Even

Diana complained that the media were more interested in her appearance than with what she was doing; or that they gave more coverage to the more frivolous activities at the expense of the ones she considered more important.) The Queen was not pleased when Diana chose the Opening of Parliament to try out a new hair style (and thereby upstaged the Queen). Gradually the couple began to accept separate engagements to avoid some of these problems. Diana continually made adjustments to ease the situation. From the beginning she switched from the high-heeled shoes she loved to flat heels so that she would not appear taller than Charles. (They are just about the same height—about 5'10".) Then, except for the black taffeta strapless formal, she selected clothing styles that, like the Queen's, were carefully non-revealing—high necks, long skirts. "The clothes are for the job," was a frequent comment. Hems needed to be weighted; hats well fastened; sleeves eased enough that she could reach up or out. Gradually she learned to wear "old" outfits to friends' weddings so she would not upstage the bride. Little wonder that she relished her nights out with friends when she could dress in tighter, sexier clothes. (In the beginning she was usually too exhausted for a night out.) Even on these occasions the paparazzi inevitably caught up with her and there were more headlines, more tears, more explanations. More grist for the mill.

Diana continued to learn more about Charles's involvement with Camilla. Her frustration with being betrayed, knowing that she was being betrayed, knowing that as a royal wife she could do nothing must have been intolerable. (*All* previous royal wives had been expected to look the other way—and did.) Her bulimia was in full swing. It kept the public guessing. Just as one reporter would "confirm" that she was indeed anorexic (her elder sister Sarah had suffered from anorexia nervosa earlier) another reporter would report that Diana had been seen eating "a whole steak and kidney pie" or a huge hamburger with fries. Little did they guess. (The stories she herself told about having to go to the "appropriate" rest room during a state dinner instead of to the nearest one should have provided a clue. Surely it is not easy to excuse one's self from a formal state dinner.) As the years went by there was more and more evidence of the growing distance between the couple. The photograph of Diana taking Charles home from the hospital following his surgery for an injury sustained in a polo accident says a lot. Reportedly, it was Camilla he wanted to cut up his food for him. Not long afterward Diana was quoted in reference to her 10th wedding anniversary, "What's to celebrate?" The Prince and Princess were no longer sharing the same bed (common practice among royalty and aristocracy, but a change for the Prince and Princess). It was really all over then, but the couple admirably continued to try to appear happy until finally, late in 1992, the Palace announced their separation. ("We didn't want to disappoint the public," said Diana.) Even so, the public, at least the romantics—and some politicians—continued to hope for reconciliation. She *should* be queen. She had worked hard and had become Britain's best "salesperson"—the best since the previous Prince of Wales, (later Edward VIII and Duke of Windsor). What she wore everybody bought. Places she visited people rushed to learn about. Causes she espoused received attention. Tourism soared. Besides that, there was the monarchy to consider. Charles would be King. His wife would be Queen. Period. Divorce was simply not an option for the heir to the throne. ("It's all right for you chaps...You can live with somebody first. I have to get it right the first time.") More importantly, perhaps, she was bringing new life into a rather out of date monarchy. She had the common touch. She restored the monarchy to the popularity it had enjoyed at the turn of the century and during the time of David, Prince of Wales, later Edward VIII and Duke of Windsor. Then came Andrew Morton's book, *Her True Story*, presumably permitted by the Princess. That ended any hope of reconciliation. Among the Royals there are three things: continuity, tradition and loyalty—and the greatest of these is loyalty. Diana had committed the unforgivable sin. When Marion Crawford ("Crawfie"), governess, tutor and friend to the then Princess Elizabeth and her sister, the Princess Margaret, published a book about her years with the little princesses, she lost her lifetime pension and her grace and favor residence. Even though there was nothing derogatory or "bad" in the book, it was considered a serious breach of confidence. As a result all those employed by the royal family are now required to sign affidavits stating that they will not publish anything about the royals. Still, Diana turned to her husband for advice (a picture of them at the funeral of Diana's grandmother shows them talking seriously), but, sadly, she was afraid to trust him.

Then late in 1995 the Queen of England, Supreme Governor of the Church of England (that officially does not condone divorce), Defender of the Faith, directed them to get a divorce—and the sooner, the better. What happened to this fairy tale marriage? What went wrong? Could it have been saved? There are, of course, no absolute answers to these questions, yet there are probabilities. From the day of the "wedding of the century" there has been an uncommon obsession with this couple, especially with the Princess—"Di-mania." There seems to have been an almost universal *need* for them to live happily ever after. Maybe, in a world that is rapidly becoming too hi-tech, a world that has discarded its heroes and fairy tales, people desperately need an old-fashioned romance, a true-life love story. Frustrated in our own lives we looked to Diana and Charles as a kind of super "soap"—a real life romance. We need assurance that *somebody* out there will live happily ever after. If we do not have heroes, we create them. So where did it go wrong? There have been a number of guesses as to why the Queen made this request, especially in such a way that it immediately became public information. The real reason is simple. She did it to help them out. They were at an impasse. Diana felt that for her to initiate divorce proceedings would make her appear to be a "bolter" like her mother, that she would be the one ending the marriage. (This would also put her at a disadvantage at the bargaining table and maybe even cause her to lose her children.) Charles felt that, as future king he could not divorce his wife, besides it would be "unchivalrous." The Queen made it possible for them to proceed with a divorce.

What went wrong? Let's take a look.

2

THE LADY DIANA SPENCER

John, youngest son of King George V and Queen Mary, brother to the future Kings Edward VIII and George VI, is mentally retarded and epileptic, probably as a result of a birth injury. This is a shameful condition and must be hidden from the public. It would not look good for the royal family to have an imperfect child. They put him away in a cottage on the grounds of Sandringham estate where his physical needs are provided for. It is for the good of England. It must be done. He dies at the age of thirteen.

The young child sat quietly but vigorously arranging and rearranging her menagerie of stuffed animals. She was very sad, but she mustn't cry. Maybe she was hungry. She reached for one of the cookies she had stashed away, but there was a lump in her throat. She put it back. The house was so quiet. Her mother was gone. She didn't know where—or why. She didn't dare ask. Everybody was angry. The servants were not talking. Her little brother was taking a nap in the nursery. She had heard them yelling—heard them yelling and yelling—heard her mummy crying—and then she was gone. Was it something she did? Maybe this scene never happened exactly like this, but similar ones surely did. The bride, Princess Diana, really was a Cinderella. She was Lady Diana Spencer, daughter of one of the oldest aristocratic families in England. She is more English than Charles (who has a high percentage of German blood). She can trace her family tree back to James I (as

Charles can). Her family has always had close ties with the royal family—serving the monarch in various capacities, having monarchs as godparents, attending each other's weddings. Diana's grandmother was lady-in-waiting to the Queen Mother. Her father was equerry to the young Queen and, earlier, to King George VI, Charles's grandfather. The Queen is godmother to Diana's brother, Charles, namesake of the Prince of Wales. Diana's sister's husband is the Queen's private secretary. Diana herself was born at Park House on the royal Sandringham property and, as a child, sometimes played with the young princes next door. Her family home, Althorp[1], is at least as imposing as Buckingham Palace. Yet, Cinderella she was. The Lady Diana Spencer, prior to and during her courtship with the Prince of Wales, supported herself by scrubbing her sister's floors and washing and ironing clothes for her sister and her sister's friends. She also was a governess and a kindergarten assistant. While these are all respectable tasks, for someone in Diana's position her behavior suggests extremely poor self-esteem. She seemed to feel that she had to *earn* love, affection, approval, by performing demeaning tasks.

Diana had a petit point pillow with the inscription, "You have to kiss a lot of frogs to find a prince," but in this case it was Diana who was transformed, almost miraculously it seems, from a slightly chubby, somewhat awkward, gauche teenager to an incredibly charming, radiant princess. The metamorphosis was not without its perils. Her first attempt at serious sophistication—the infamous black taffeta strapless gown designed by the Emanuels was a big mistake—and Charles did not help by remarking that "royals only wear black for funerals." This was her first real test of meeting society as a royal and she needed all the confidence she could muster. (She was still nineteen.) Charles was no help. Princess Grace of Monaco, once a commoner herself, saw her distress and came to her rescue. "Don't worry," she told her. "It gets worse." Sadly, Princess Grace did not live to see how much worse. Not surprisingly Diana was next seen in a very demure pastel gown with gloves reaching to the sleeves (but she had made her point).

Diana Frances Spencer was born July 1, 1961. There was nothing especially newsworthy about her birth. She was the third daughter in a family desperate for a male heir. Born on the Sandringham Estate, she was christened in Sandringham Church and had well-to-do commoners for godparents. When her brother finally arrived three years later, he was christened at Westminster Abbey with the Queen as principal godparent. (Her sisters also had royal godparents—the Queen Mother for Sarah, the Duke of Kent for Jane.) By the time Diana was born the marriage of her parents was already in trouble. They divorced when she was six years old. Divorce was rare at that time and especially in her family's social set. Only one of her friends had parents who were also divorced. Diana's mother had fully expected to have custody of her children. However, her father countersued, citing adultery, and won—with the help of Diana's grandmother. Her mother's own mother testified against her because, royalist and snobbish, she believed her grandchildren would be better off living with an aristocrat, even an abusive one, than with a commoner. She also was horrified that her daughter would embarrass one of the Queen's courtiers, of whom Diana's father was one. She swore that she never witnessed Johnny's physical violence. Perhaps she really had not. Domestic violence was considered shameful in those days and hidden at all costs. Frances never forgave her mother.[2] Diana's mother appears to have been a very strong willed woman, at least when she was young. Over the years her spirit seems to have been broken. Diana's father was actually engaged to marry someone else when Frances Roche, a beautiful young debutante, met him. She was not deterred. They were subsequently engaged and their marriage was the "wedding of the year," celebrated in Westminster Abbey (perhaps another reason Charles and Diana chose St. Paul's Cathedral) and among the guests were the Queen, Prince Philip and the Queen Mother. When life with the Earl Spencer palled, his wife left him to marry wealthy wallpaper heir Peter Shand-Kydd, creating a terrific scandal. In defense of Diana's mother, it should be noted that she was only twenty-five when Diana, her fourth child, was born.

Prior to that she had been pressured to have tests done to determine why she "was unable to have sons." This must have been extremely humiliating. Her third child was a son who only lived a few hours. Who can measure the effect of such a loss? It was only after she had born a healthy son, Diana's brother Charles, that she left. Perhaps she felt she had done her duty. Also Diana's father was physically and verbally abusive—as his father had been.

Diana did not do well in school, actually becoming the equivalent of a high school dropout. This is not surprising given that her family was falling apart. Beset by feelings of abandonment and fear of further loss, there is little wonder that she found it difficult to concentrate on her studies. It is during these formative years that so much of the personality develops. Trust is basic. When her mother left and her father retreated to his study, Diana felt betrayed, abandoned, isolated. She also was burdened with guilt, feeling that she was the cause of the marital breakdown. At this young age children perceive and believe themselves to be the center of the universe and that they cause whatever happens. So she was left to believe that if only she had been "better"—if she had been a boy perhaps, her family—her security—would not have been fractured. What if she lost even more? What if her father left—or her beloved baby brother died—like her other brother? She must be *very* good. She must stay out of the way and not upset anybody. Her sister, Sarah, was the closest thing she had to a mother, so she must, at all costs, "keep" her. Very early she learned that you can't really trust anybody (and every time she tried she proved it all over again) and you must always do what people want—or they won't keep you.

Such deep insecurities are almost impossible to overcome. She comforted herself with her stuffed animals and with her baby brother, whom she mothered—and with food. Even that produced more guilt. She would often hear him crying for his "Mummy" at night. Sometimes she would go to his room and comfort him, but more often she was too afraid of the dark and she didn't go. She only lay awake and felt guilty. For years she insisted on having a night light on, so fearful was she of the dark. When she went away to school, she was allowed one stuffed animal. She painted its eyes with luminescent paint so he "could see her at night." Away at school her anxieties increased, even though by now they were largely subconscious. Her need to be home to be sure that she still had a home made it difficult for her to concentrate. Not doing well in her studies only led to more anxiety, guilt and fear—she was *supposed* to do well. Her sisters and her brother were all good students. It was expected of her. She compensated by excelling in areas that required less concentration—or at least a different kind—her diving, her dancing, her love of animals and children and of older people. She learned early to talk her way out of an awkward situation. She became quite creative in this. It proved to be both an asset and a liability in later years. In addition to everything else Diana was a "middle child." Her sisters were older and more sophisticated; her brother was not only the baby of the family, but also the son and heir. Diana moved into her teens feeling she was not much good at—or for—anything. She was fourteen when she moved from the relatively cozy home at Sandringham to the palatial, almost scary, Althorp (pronounced *altrup*) mansion. Her father's remarriage and involvement with his new wife took away any security she had left. Her only value, in her mind, was her aristocratic status, but since most of her peer group had similar status that was not a lot of help. Photos of her as a child and early teenager show a solemn pensive child. She spent a lot of time alone. Her favorite pastimes were swimming (she was "famous" for her diving), ballet (she grew too tall to follow this dream), and reading Barbara Cartland's romantic novels. Lonely, insecure, filled with "happily ever after" stories, little wonder that she day dreamed about the Prince of Wales, whose picture happened to hang over her bed at school—her knight in shining armor who would rescue her, love, cherish and protect her for life. Diana frequently referred to herself as "thick as a plank," yet obviously she could not possibly have done what she did unless she was quite bright. In addition to managing a family and two royal homes with large staff, she had to learn a tremendous amount of information about various heads of states, the countries she visited, the diverse groups with which she met. She had to learn to deal with an increasingly aggressive press and the paparazzi and always, always do the proper thing in every situation. That she was amazingly successful was shown by her being equally at home with a movie star, a young mother, an AIDS victim, or a head of state. What we did not see was the anger and fear, the stress, tears and frustration of trying to do more than she was able to do.

After her mother left—an action Diana, as a child, could only perceive as abandonment—her father, hurt and confused, retreated into his own world, leaving Diana feeling bereft of both parents. Nannies and governesses came and went with alarming regularity so that she was not even able to establish a lasting relationship with a surrogate parent. Eventually, Raine, Countess of Dartmouth (daughter of romance novelist, Barbara Cartland) "took [the Earl] in hand," married him (providing the proverbial fairy-tale stepmother) and immediately began to renovate Althorp, the Spencer estate, to pay off the enormous death taxes then due. Diana and her sisters and brother did not appreciate her efforts. Diana's older sisters were away at boarding school. That left only her little brother and Diana "mothered" him. It is no coincidence that she has continued to enjoy working with young children. Diana seems almost to have raised herself. She never lacked for material things, both her grandmothers helped out, and certainly she was loved by both her parents—but nobody was *there*. Christmases and birthdays were exercises in extravagance, with each parent trying to outdo the other in gift giving. Diana has been quoted as saying that she was "supposed to be a boy." Given young children's sense that the world revolves around them, we can assume that Diana thought that her parents' marriage fell apart, her mother left and her father retreated into his own world because she was not the son they had hoped for. She was not "right." So she tried very hard to be as good as she possibly could so that she would be loved—or maybe so that she would be *kept*.

Reportedly she and her brother frequently visited the grave of their older brother and wondered if either of them would have even been born if their brother John had lived. In families such as the Spencers a male heir is as important as it is in royal families. So here is Diana, sixteen years old, expected to maintain the family status, perhaps even help overcome the stigma of divorce with its bitter custody battle. Her sister Jane seems to have been fairly supportive, but it was Sarah whom Diana wanted to emulate—maybe because it was harder to win Sarah's approval—and so she dressed like her, cleaned her house, washed and ironed her clothes, sometimes dated her former boyfriends (of whom Charles was one).

Then came the fateful day when she met Prince Charles "in the middle of a plowed field" on a shooting weekend at Althorp. Technically, this was not the first meeting, but it was the one that counted.

Diana, still a teenager, used to considerable freedom, was relatively unsophisticated and naive. She had not had a serious relationship before. She was young, romantic (Barbara Cartland, the mother of her stepmother supplied her with copies of each of her romantic novels), in love and very vulnerable. She, like her mother, was also strong willed, as she would have to be to survive. While Charles's life style barely changed—he still played polo, hunted at Sandringham and Balmoral, went skiing in Switzerland, spent weekends with his friends—Diana's lifestyle changed drastically and totally. The pattern was set during the unusual (to us commoners) courtship. Charles essentially did what he had done all along and with other girl friends. It was Diana who had to use all kinds of subterfuge (climbing out back windows, using a flatmate for a decoy, taking the bus, switching cars with her grandmother) to get to the designated meeting place. One of the first press photos of her is very telling. She is leaving Princess Margaret's birthday party alone. That she has been with the Prince is obvious from her flat heel evening slippers. Over her pink chiffon evening gown she is wearing the same warm green coat that she wears to work. Never did he send a car for her, much less pick her up personally. (This was, no doubt, an attempt to avoid publicity. Nevertheless, the effect was the same. She was expected to look out for herself.) This very subterfuge probably added excitement, perhaps allowing the teenage Diana to overlook or disregard more serious issues or considerations. Diana and Charles had very little time alone or in "normal" situations. For the sake of propriety they were almost always with a group or a chaperone—and that group seemed to always include the Parker-Bowleses.[3] As soon as he proposed[4] she left for Australia for a much needed break. Soon after the announcement of the engagement at the end of February he left for a five week tour. There were several shorter trips. In only five months she had to learn basic protocol and begin to learn how to be a royal. She had to put together a royal wardrobe, decorate and furnish two royal homes and prepare to star in the wedding of the century—a formidable task in itself. He had his royal duties to attend to. (However, she began to be included in many of these.) Early pictures in Tetbury and Broadlands show a happy couple. She looks very nervous (and not very chic) in her first balcony appearance.

There have been various stories about Diana's training for the role of Princess—so many, in fact, that one wonders if she really had any training at all. (Obviously she did. In a few short months she had to learn who should curtsy to her and to whom she should curtsy—royal protocol is extremely complicated—and a million other details.) Immediately after he "popped the question" Diana said, "Yes, please." Still Charles insisted that she take a few weeks to consider. (Did he want Diana to be sure or did he still need time to consider?) At her mother's suggestion Diana traveled to Australia to be with her mother and stepfather for a brief respite. By all accounts Charles only called her once, his beloved fiancée during that time and not until she had tried several times to call him. Nor did he meet her on her return. Before the engagement was officially announced Diana was moved into Clarence House, the home of the Queen Mother so that she would have the protection of the Palace. (This time a Rolls-Royce was sent to pick her up—and she was assigned a protection officer.) She would shortly move into Buckingham Palace where she would live until the day before the wedding. It was deemed "inappropriate" for bride and groom to emerge from the same house enroute to the wedding, even if that "house" was Buckingham Palace. Again, neither her fiancé nor the Queen Mother greeted her on her arrival in what surely was an almost overwhelming world. There was, however, a note from Camilla Parker-Bowles, welcoming her and inviting her to lunch. (Welcoming her to *what*?) Camilla and her husband had been present at most of the weekend parties at the homes of friends which made up the courtship of Charles and Diana. Even with her lack of experience in courtship, and knowing a royal courtship is probably different, Diana still sensed that something was not quite right. But she was very much in love, and she was marrying the Prince of Wales.[5] One day she would be Queen of England. Very few women in all history have had that title. Heady stuff for a teenager with low self-esteem. It was simpler to overlook the nagging doubts.

Then there was the tremendous task of planning and preparing for the wedding of the century. Soon after the engagement was announced, Charles left for a five week tour in Australia and New Zealand, leaving her alone in a strange world. How does a nineteen year old manage? Who was guiding her? She says, "Suddenly my mother and I had to go and buy six of everything," yet she seems to have been making most of the decisions. Her mother was helping her with guest lists; her sisters were there to provide advice. Jane, having worked for *Vogue*, put her in touch with Anna Harvey on the *Vogue* staff to assist with basic wardrobe details. Contact with her friends was limited once she moved into Buckingham Palace. In addition to the wedding and honeymoon outfits, she must have a royal wardrobe, one that would allow for three or four changes per day, for all kinds of occasions and all kinds of weather. (Just a few of the occasions before the wedding included a society wedding, four days of Ascot, several charity functions, Charles's obligatory visits, the multitude of pre-wedding teas, luncheons and dinners.) Diana had almost nothing suitable ("one long dress, a silk shirt and one pair of smart shoes," she recalls). For her dates with the Prince she had ransacked the closets of her friends and sisters. Still, with all the help and assistance, it was Diana who had to make the final decisions. Charles, on whom she was depending for guidance, was gone a good part of this time. Certainly, the time in Australia was spent making guest lists, considering wardrobe requirements, and other wedding considerations, but these would have been very preliminary plans. Diana appears to have chosen the Emanuels to create her wedding gown on her own. She needed to borrow an outfit for an official photograph. Someone supplied a "lacy pink and cream confection" which she learned had been designed by the Emanuels. She decided to talk to them about her wedding dress. (They also created the black taffeta strapless dress that created so much attention.) Her mother did help her select her engagement ensemble (an "off the peg" from Harrod's) and suggested an interior decorator, Dudley Poplek. Diana had lunch with her sisters two days before the wedding and dinner with Jane on her wedding eve. Fifteen years later, Andrew Morton, describing the new look of her sitting room lists photographs of her father, her sisters and her brother. There is no mention of her mother. Her relationship with her mother appears to have been very off and on (yet her mother apparently was there for her during the wedding preparations, at least part of the time.) She had a wealth of resources and technical assistance, but she was *nineteen*—and a "young" nineteen at that. She probably had never even worn a hat. Charles took an active part in choosing St. Paul's Cathedral instead of the traditional Westminster Abbey and in selecting and organizing the music. Certainly the Queen was involved and wanted to make sure everything went smoothly and looked good to all the important guests and the rest of the world. Actually Diana had very little input into the wedding itself, which was a state event.[6] Still she had to handle personal aspects. On the one hand she seems to have had almost no say-so at all—it was a state affair—but her personal part had to be perfect and must meet the standards expected of royalty. She wanted desperately to get it right. She had to make a *drastic* transition from the teenager with casual clothes, no make-up and little jewelry to royal princess in a very short. time. She had to learn in a few months what Charles and his parents had been learning from birth. Who helped her? The Queen's Lady-in-Waiting, Susan Hussey, was assigned to assist her in learning protocol. Sir Edward Adeane, the Prince's Private Secretary was available. Sir Everett Oliver was recalled from Madrid and offered a position as private secretary to the Princess. She is also overseeing the decorating and staffing of two royal homes. (She has a very competent interior decorator, still all the final decisions are hers—and she needs to use as many wedding gifts as will fit.) How many nineteen year olds can do this, even with plenty of money and staff? Add to this that she overhears Charles talking fondly to Camilla ("I will always love you," he told her—had he said as much to Diana?), that she insists on opening what she thinks (hopes?) is a wedding gift only to discover that it is in fact a gift from Charles—to Camilla, which he delivers personally two days before the wedding. But Diana is said to have been reassured when he sent (sent?) her a signet ring with an "affectionate" note the night before the wedding. Apparently he did not see her or even phone her on their wedding eve. And they are not even married yet.

The wedding day must have been exhausting, but it was finally over and they were away on their fabulous honeymoon. It was not, however, exactly, a honeymoon suite in the Poconos. The Prince took along books by his friend and mentor, Sir Laurens van der Post, for them to read and discuss over lunch. They had little time really alone together. A crew and staff of over 270 men and one woman, Diana's dresser—and Camilla—accompanied them. They dressed for dinner every night—black tie, with selected officers, the Royal Marine Band playing nearby. (Camilla was along in the form of photos falling from an appointment book and new cuff links with hers and Charles's initials intertwined.) Diana's bulimia, which began during the build-up to the wedding, worsened on the cruise.

Only much later did we learn that he spent his wedding eve night with Camilla.[7]

3

CHARLES, PRINCE OF WALES

The King, aware of the growing hostility of the English toward the Germans, sheds his German Sax-Coburg-Gotha skin for the more acceptable name of Windsor. In desperation his cousin, the Czar of Russia, appeals to him for asylum for him and his family. Fearful that the Czar's German wife might prove embarrassing—make him appear more German, weaken his own position, he refuses them asylum. They may, however, deposit their riches in English banks. Subsequently the Czar, along with his entire family, is brutally murdered by the Russian Revolutionaries. George V is saddened, but he understands that he must do what is best for England.

His full title is His Royal Highness, the Prince Charles Philip Arthur George, Prince of Wales and Earl of Chester, Duke of Cornwall and Rothesay, Earl of Carrick and Baron of Renfrew, Lord of the Isles and Great Steward of Scotland, Knight of the Garter. He signs his name *Charles*. Charles, Prince of Wales, was the world's most eligible bachelor.[1] Charles, too, has never lacked for material things. He was born, just after the end of World War II, to Princess Elizabeth and Philip, Duke of Edinburgh. England was still reeling from the devastation of the war. He grew up in Buckingham Palace, spent vacations in various other royal residences. His mother, the Princess Elizabeth had been heir to the throne since age ten. (When her Uncle David, Edward VIII, abdicated, her father became king and she became heiress apparent.) Even before that she was treated as heir since her Uncle David had no children and it was assumed that she would succeed him. While being primed for the responsibility of monarch, she, with her sister Margaret, led remarkably cloistered and sheltered lives, largely because they were royal, but also because of the war. Cosseted and protected as only a princess can be, still the mantle of royal responsibility fell heavily on her young shoulders.[2] Due to the constant bombing of London and the ever-present threat of invasion the Princesses were virtually isolated at Windsor Castle for much of their formative years.

The Queen was only thirteen when she met the handsome young Naval Cadet, Philip of Greece, and fell in love. (As with Charles and Diana, this was not their first meeting, but it was the one that counted.) Philip, only five years older, was eons older in experience. He was literally a man without a country—or much of anything else. He was a Greek prince without a throne. His parents were divorced and his father was unable to care for his family. His mother was deaf from the age of four. He had literally been passed from relative to relative throughout his childhood and youth. A stable home was something he wanted badly. His sisters married men with high positions in the Nazi government. His salvation lay in the fact that his mother's brother was the well-known, powerful Lord Louis Mountbatten, Earl of Burma, Viceroy of India and Admiral of the Fleet, who saw early the benefits of marriage between his royal nephew and the future Queen of England. While Elizabeth's father had genuine concerns about his daughter's marriage to someone with such close connections to the Nazis,[3] Elizabeth was determined. Philip seems never to have questioned his destiny. He seemed to be quite content playing childish games with the Princesses Elizabeth and Margaret and then, going on to his more adult entertainment. While he has not always been faithful, he has always been totally committed to the Queen, to the Monarch. He, too, was born royal. He seems to have been the one person most opposed to the Margaret-Townsend marriage (aside from her mother, that is), probably because he feared the scandal might tarnish the image of the young Queen. He was—and is—a man of great pride, yet he married Princess Elizabeth knowing that, once she was Queen, for the rest of his life he would be required to walk, literally, in her shadow. (He did not know it would be so soon.) Officially, he walks four paces behind the Queen. His lowest point was probably the day the young Queen, on advice of her counselors, decreed that her children would be known as Windsors, not Mountbattens, although this was later amended somewhat. ("I'm just a bloody amoeba!" he screamed.) Actually, both names had been Anglicized from their original German and Mountbatten was not even Philip's name, but had been his mother's name.[4] Elizabeth was shrewd enough, even with her lack of experience, to recognize how galling Philip's role could be and so she compensated when she could and especially made sure that he was head of the family. This was no hardship. She adored her handsome husband and leaned heavily on him. He taught the sheltered Princess about life—nightclubs, movies, all the ordinary experiences she had missed. She did not interfere with his decisions concerning the children's education. The result for Charles was that he had an authoritarian father with high expectations and a mother who was not really there for him. (However, the Queen Mother has said that the Queen was the stricter disciplinarian and that Philip tried to "soften" the effect.)

Although she breastfed her infant son for a short while, thereafter she saw him twice a day, a half-hour in the morning and an hour in the evening, when she was not on an official tour or with Philip, who was still in the Royal Navy. Charles's parents made a real effort to give him a more "normal" upbringing than either of them had. He was sent to public school (British equivalent of private school)—first to Hill House, Knightsbridge, then to Cheam, and finally to his father's school of Gordonstoun with its Spartan discipline designed to build masculine character. The Queen and her sister had been tutored in the palace. Queen Mary, aware of what lay ahead for her, tried to remedy her inadequate curriculum, but the Queen's mother felt strongly that the young Princess should have the same kind of education that she, herself, had had, which was intended to prepare her to be the wife of a royal or aristocratic husband. It did not prepare her to be a monarch. The Queen was very much aware that her education had not been adequate. The Prince's parents, especially Prince Philip, wanted him to "go to school with other boys of his generation and to learn to live with other children...[to absorb] the discipline imposed by education with other children." Eventually he obtained a degree from Trinity College, Cambridge, the first heir to the throne to actually earn a degree. He also spent a year at Timbertop in Australia (his equerry said, "I went out with a boy and returned with a man") and attended one term at Welsh College at Aberystwyth to study Welsh history, culture and language prior to his investiture as Prince of Wales. Bonnie Prince Charles was a cherubic child, solemn and round-faced. Not for him the rambunctiousness of his sister Anne (his father's favorite)—and later his own son William, nor the imperialism his mother had often shown as a child. Although well cared for, Charles, like Diana, had grown up feeling lonely and inadequate. His mother became Queen when he was just three years old and even before that, as a result of her father's poor health, had undertaken many royal duties including official tours which kept her away from her children for weeks and even months at a time. In addition, she was a navy wife and, as much as possible, went to wherever her husband was, leaving Charles in the competent care of governesses and his grandparents. The story is told that on one occasion Charles shook hands with his mother after her return from an extended tour, and then turned back to his governess. There is, in fact, a well-publicized news photo of the Queen touching him on the shoulder—or straightening his collar—after one such trip. (The Queen herself, as a young child, cried bitterly when taken from her nanny by the mother who had missed her so.) The Queen managed the almost impossible task of keeping the British Monarchy alive and well long after most of the rest of the world has learned to live without kings and queens. She is portrayed as only a figurehead with no real power[5]—and not too bright, sometimes described as "dowdy." Actually she has tremendous power and knows how to use it. She has multiplied her inheritance several times over. It has been said that her children "can do no wrong," yet it must have seemed to the young Charles that her husband and the monarchy came ahead of him. Still, he is heir to her crown and has surely been molded, in part at least, by her life and behavior. She is totally regal. Like her grandmother, Queen Mary, the Queen never shows her distress in public. (If she cried when her beloved father died only Philip knew—and certainly she showed no distress over the death of Diana, Princess of Wales.) Nor does she voice opinions on anything that can be considered politically controversial.

As he was growing up Charles was a constant disappointment to his father who wanted the shy, sensitive, introverted boy to be more "masculine," more athletic. Over the years Charles "proved" himself over and over in an effort to win his father's approval and admiration. As Diana came to know Charles she sensed the lonely little boy in him and instinctively responded to that part of him. As always, she wanted to ease the pain and loneliness, to "make it better." Undoubtedly, she, Cinderella, also responded to Prince Charming, the Prince of Wales. Probably not even Diana could separate her love for Charles the man from her love for Charles, Prince of Wales. Here, she felt, was someone who would love her and protect her, someone who could supply the love and security that she felt had been lacking all her life. She perceived him as larger than life and was totally in awe of him, formally calling him "Sir" until they were officially engaged.

Prince Philip, whatever his faults—and he had some—was totally loyal to the Queen. Charles also had learned to expect this. (Diana was very loyal for a long time—and Philip was not always faithful.) Philip's contribution to the monarchy, incidentally, has been greatly underestimated in the opinion of this writer. If he must walk always in the Queen's shadow (four steps behind her), he was also the wind beneath her wings. He shared her burdens of office. Surprisingly, she did not share the official "red boxes"[6] with him as most of her predecessors had done. It would have eased his sense of being only "an appendage." He was her eyes and ears, since he could go where she could not and could speak out when she could not. He provided emotional support as well as information and advice. She adored him. Charles had also learned to expect that. From infancy, his every need was anticipated and catered to, as it continued to be in adulthood. Reportedly, he does not even put his own freshly ironed money into his billfold or the toothpaste on his toothbrush. It was the only way of life he had known and hardly prepared him for real life marriage and fatherhood. His "job" has not helped. On Prince William's birth certificate his occupation is listed as "Prince of the United Kingdom," yet, as he has explained, there is no constitutional role for the heir to the throne. Some internships last for weeks or months—maybe a year. His has gone on for almost half a century. That is a long time to tread water. He has attempted to be seen as champion of the poor, but lives the most privileged of lives so he lacks credibility.

It was tempting to rejoice in the union of these two people who so needed each other. Yet psychologists know that two emotionally needy people can rarely help each other. Neither has to give what the other needs. Empty pitchers cannot fill one another.

Charles has been taught all his life that he is the second most important person in the world (his mother being first). Before other children are ready for school he had his own car, chauffeur, valet and detective. Everything and everyone in his world revolved around him. To his credit, he was never arrogant in the usual sense of the word, still "normal" to him was being totally catered to. Also, he was mostly in the care of women—his nanny, his governess, his grandmother. Both parents were often away but he seemed to see even less of his father than of his mother. To offset this, his father, a very masculine man, sent him to the harsh, discipline building schools he himself had attended. (Also, fearing he would be spoiled by so much attention, Philip saw his own role as counteracting the spoiling.) Charles, a shy, introverted child, was miserable at school and once he was able to, he made sure he would never be in such a position again. (It should also be noted that, although he poured out his woes in letters to his grandmother, he stayed the course.) Once out of school, he surrounded himself with loyal aides and advisors who understood his position, who catered to him, "yes" men, sycophants. At least he thought they were loyal. When Charles's Great-uncle, Edward VIII, abdicated, he (Edward) discovered to his dismay that *his* "loyal" supporters were not so loyal after all. They fled like rats from a sinking ship.

Where women were concerned Charles was a late bloomer. Although, by his own admission, he "fell in love easily," he inherited little of his father's suave charm (although he was pleasant and charming enough). He was teased all his life about his big ears (his mother's first comment on seeing his first son was, "Thank goodness, he doesn't have his father's ears!") and he did not develop his strong physique until after his school days. But he had a title. He was the future King of England. This made him very attractive to women (although few of them actually wanted to marry him—that was *too* much responsibility). As a result he began to be more comfortable with the fairer sex and even to fancy himself somewhat of a ladies' man, someone a lady would consider it a privilege to be seen with.

Charles met Camilla Shand in 1971. She was the girlfriend of his friend Andrew Parker-Bowles, but—in the royal way—just as, two generations earlier, Jamie Stuart stepped away for Bertie, so Andrew stepped aside for his royal friend. Interestingly, although Charles appeared to be smitten with her, she was never labeled his "girl friend"—and their meetings never made it to the popular press at that time even though the media were constantly on the look-out for a possible royal bride. Several writers have said that Camilla would have married him in a minute, but he never proposed. He "dithered." Charles is a ditherer, no question about it, but there are other considerations. First of all, it is very unlikely that Camilla wanted to be Queen.[7] Nothing about her suggests that she would fit into that role, in that spotlight. She enjoys the country life, the hunting, but the court life with all its ritual and special dress was not for her. Secondly, although there were "sparks," Charles, especially in his twenties, aside from his title and position, probably did not sweep women off their feet. He was still shy and diffident, much more like his mother than his suave, charismatic father who charmed women around the world. She was much more attracted to the debonair Andrew. From the Prince's perspective, although she certainly knew how to get his attention, he was far from ready to settle down with a wife (was he *ever* ready?), and she simply did not meet the requirements for Princess of Wales. Given his Victorian upbringing he might even have considered her unfit to be the mother of the future king. A virgin bride she would not be. She married Andrew Parker-Bowles (who has close ties to the royal family) and asked Charles to be godfather to her first child, a son named Thomas (mentioned in the "Camillagate" tapes). Still, their paths continued to cross, rather frequently actually, and although they were sometimes seen together, no one paid any attention. She simply was not the kind of woman for the media to get excited about. She was almost always included in whatever group Charles and Diana were with and even gave her approval to the marriage,[8] describing Diana as a "mouse" and not seeing her as a threat to her own relationship with the Prince. Many weekends were spent at Bolehyde Manor, the country home of the Parker-Bowleses. Based on the Camillagate tapes, their relationship apparently flourished—yet he had a duty to marry a young woman and produce an heir. Camilla is only a year older than Charles, but she "mothers" him—something he craves. If Charles truly intended to end the affair, it is certain that Camilla never did. (Reportedly Prince Philip extracted a promise from Charles that he would discontinue his relationship with Camilla for at least five years, to give his marriage a chance—and have an heir. If so, it is a promise that was never kept—and one Camilla never made.)

In the final weeks before the wedding Charles began to sense the walls closing in on him. He knew it was his duty to marry and produce an heir, but Diana could be difficult at times. She had her own ideas about the wedding—and the guest list. She was losing weight at an alarming rate and at times would burst into tears for no apparent reason. He didn't know what to do. He liked his quiet, regimented life, surrounded by people whose sole responsibility was to cater to his needs, whatever they were. Not only did he see marriage as a tremendous responsibility—it meant he must give up his comforter. The longer he put it off, the more awesome it became. His sister never cried. His mother, the Queen, never cried. His mistress, Camilla, never cried. Camilla...Camilla would know what to do. She would comfort him. He sent Diana a signet ring to match his own and an affectionate note—then he sent for Camilla.[9] So Charles took up his position in St. Paul's Cathedral on his wedding day with his own twenty-five foot train. He was trailing a full-fledged enduring relationship with another woman, leaving little space for his new bride.

4

QUEEN ELIZABETH, THE QUEEN MOTHER

Conspirator?

I am no conspirator! I have not conspired. But as the centre of a traitorous plot, that will not save me! Now I know fear indeed. I take to my bed, knowing that even though I might crawl into a mousehole they will seek me out. And so they have. Mary must clear the way for her Spanish Prince. Little help now that I am the Princess Elizabeth, daughter of the mighty Henry VIII. I wait—and wait—for weeks—locked in my Whitehall lodgings—until finally I hear the words: "It is the Queen's high will and pleasure that you be committed to the Tower." My sister Mary believes I am a threat to her throne and her happiness. I am her prisoner. It is for the good of England. It must be.

When the engagement was announced, Diana moved into the protection of the Queen Mother's home, Clarence House, and then into Buckingham Palace. It was generally assumed that the Queen Mother, with all her years experience in "royalese" took her under her wing and coached her in all things royal. Diana has said this did not happen. As the Waleses's marital problems worsened, Diana felt the Queen Mother always took Charles's side, blaming her for the problems and so she was not comfortable with her. Diana was perhaps supersensitive, but Charles was the Queen Mother's favorite grandchild and he depended on her for the emotional support he did not always receive from his parents. Also, the grandmother who had betrayed Diana's mother during the divorce and custody hearings, causing her to lose her children—of whom Diana was one—was the Queen Mother's closest friend, so Diana felt, right or wrong, that the cards were already stacked against her. "She did a real hatchet job on me," she was to say later, speaking of her own grandmother.

Diana and the Queen Mother had much in common. Both were aristocratic commoners who married sons of monarchs. Both had amazing charisma and seemed to effortlessly charm any crowd or individual. Both flourished in the spotlight, draining though it might be at times. Both appeared feminine and demure, but were strong willed. Both were people pleasers. The Queen Mother's compulsive need to please kept her Victorian and traditional; Diana's need to please took her to the ill and needy—these were the ones who responded with lavish praise and affection. Both knew what they wanted and were not afraid to go for it. What was different was their relationships with their husbands. Charles, Prince of Wales, and Bertie, Duke of York and future King George VI (as well as Bertie's older brother David, Prince of Wales, later King Edward VIII and Duke of Windsor) were men who were dominated and intimidated by their fathers and who had lacked a nurturing mother. Both had spent time with nurturing grandmothers, so they knew what they were missing. They wanted—craved—the warm, loving home life they never had. Both women sensed this in their husbands and used it to their advantage. The Queen Mother was able to fill this need for Bertie (as Wallis Simpson did for David). Diana, on the other hand, was marrying a man who was much older, much more experienced than she. She was looking to him as a father figure, someone who would provide *her* with the love and security she had never known. It was Camilla who provided the mothering. Charles was not nearly so damaged as his grandfather had been, even though his childhood was lonely and his parents had little time for him due to the pressures of their royal responsibilities. Still he had never been abused or physically neglected.

He had good governesses; he was sent to public (private) school (as opposed to being educated at home as all previous heirs to the throne had been). He had also, by the time he married Diana, gained considerable confidence, at least on the surface, simply through experience. The big difference was that Bertie adored Elizabeth; Charles loved another woman. That is quite a difference. There was another important difference. The Queen Mother had grown up in a warm, close-knit, fun loving family. This was one of the things that attracted Bertie. He wanted a home like that, so different from what he had known. The Queen Mother had been taught from birth to believe that she was "special" and deserved the best of everything. This gave her a special kind of confidence. She also had the firm support of her mother-in-law, who saw her as an ally in developing the Duke's potential. Diana, on the other hand, while also having a title, never had the security of a warm loving cohesive family unit. She had the same kind of confidence Charles had, based on proper training and social status, but both lacked real self-esteem. They judged themselves by how others perceived them. Diana, sadly, did not trust her own mother and she felt the Queen would "be on Charles's side." She truly felt isolated.

Elizabeth Bowes-Lyon, youngest daughter of the Earl and Countess Strathmore, was a charming, overindulged child who grew up into an even more charming young lady who was witty, funny, and flirtatious. She was often described as "dainty and feminine"—qualities which were very much valued in the early part of the century, qualities which she nurtured, but they covered a will of iron. The young man she set her heart on (one Jamie Stuart—perhaps a descendent of the Jamie Stuart who became James I?) chose someone else—with a little nudging from Bertie's mom, so she hid her hurt and turned her attention to the most eligible bachelor in the world, David, Prince of Wales. Born to be King, his charm captivated his subjects around the world. He was the most popular Prince of Wales ever and not until Diana's entry into the family would the British royal family enjoy such popularity again. His brother, Bertie, meanwhile, had fallen desperately in love with the charming Elizabeth (while she was trying to charm the Prince of Wales). Bertie was not nearly so desirable. Both boys had been seriously emotionally damaged by abuse and neglect during infancy and early childhood, but it showed more with Bertie. (When it was discovered the nanny was promptly "put away," but the damage had already been done.) He was nervous, shy, sickly, had a bad stutter, and nervous tics. He was uncomfortable in social settings. However, as luck—or fate—would have it, in 1923, the *Daily News* announced that David would marry Elizabeth. (Names were not used, but identity was clear. Where *did* they get this information?) She waited for his reaction. It was not long in coming. He immediately authorized his staff to issue an official denial. Although, so far as is known, David had never led her to believe that he was considering marriage with her (he was not considering marriage with *anyone* at that time), she took this as a public rejection, extremely humiliating—and she never forgave him. Keep this in mind. It affected history. Having been turned down by the man she loved and by the man she wanted, she took another look at Bertie (she was already twenty-three, "elderly" for maidens in those days) and saw some qualities most others had overlooked. What she saw was a man who, except for his nervous habits, was really not unattractive. He was physically fit. His dress was meticulous; he looked especially good in uniform. He was, after all, second in line for the throne. She would not be queen, but if David never married, which some thought likely, she would one day be first lady of the land. Even if he did marry, she would be near the top. Lesser women would curtsy to her. And Bertie adored her. She decided that she could make him into the man she wanted. She did all that and more. She made him King.

To her credit, once she decided to accept his proposal she was totally and forever committed. With her charming smile, her unique wave ("like unscrewing a jar lid," she told the young Diana), and her "I know, I know," adjusted in tone to the specific situation, she won the hearts of the people. As "The Queen Mum" she was beloved and venerated by the masses. With the possible exception of Princess Diana, she consistently remained the most popular of the royals. With her support and encouragement—she actually accompanied Bertie to sessions with a speech therapist and made sure his speeches were written in such a way as to minimize his difficulty—he became a much beloved and respected king. During World War II the royal family endeared itself to the people, especially of London, but also throughout the world, by refusing to flee to safety. London was being bombed to smithereens by the Germans at this time. Nine million buildings were destroyed. The Princesses were relatively safe in their isolation at Windsor Castle. They would have been safer in Canada. King George VI and his charming consort Queen Elizabeth were frequently seen inspecting the bomb damage and comforting the people. They became a symbol of hope and survival when England had little else. When asked if she thought it appropriate to wear her fine clothes and jewels into these areas, she replied, "Of course. If they were coming to see me they would wear their best clothes." It was typical of her almost uncanny ability to say the right thing, to make the appropriate gesture.

But before she could make him a *good* king, she had to make him a *king*. When she decided to accept his marriage proposal she was resigned to being a Duchess, not a Queen, but when there were questions about the Prince of Wales's mistress, when he made it clear that he intended to marry Wallis Simpson, a twice married American woman,[1] still legally married to her second husband, Elizabeth saw her chance. She was already on good terms with king makers Major Andrew Hardinge and Sir Alan Lascelles. (Elizabeth and Helen Hardinge were close friends.) In her unassuming way she encouraged them to encourage the new king to abdicate. He must choose between the crown and the woman he loved, he was told. This was not quite true—but David was new at being King and still suffered from his father's hypercritical attitude[2] He depended on his advisors, who were being supported and influenced by Elizabeth, probably even much more than they themselves realized. He chose the woman he loved.

David and Bertie parted on the best of terms (but not Elizabeth, whom he insisted not be present at his farewell dinner with his mother, Queen Mary, and his brothers). He was to marry abroad and remain abroad for about two years, after which time he believed he would return and be "assistant" to the King, as Bertie would have been to him had he remained king. He was never allowed to return except for such occasions as the funerals of his brother and his mother (but not to the family dinner following the funeral) and his niece's coronation—even then he was asked not to bring his wife—she would not be "received."[3] (He did return with her privately for medical treatment. Interestingly, it was on one such trip that the Duchess's jewels—royal heirloom jewels, gifts from the Duke, were stolen. Scotland Yard investigated, but they were never found.)[4] By all accounts it was Elizabeth who prevented his return. She not only prevented his return to England, she interfered with any meaningful work outside of England. Most excruciating of all, she prevented his wife from ever having the title of "Her Royal Highness," even though as the legal wife of "His Royal Highness," she had every right to it. It was Elizabeth who insisted on eliminating all his supporters, beginning with Major Hardinge, who had actually expedited the overthrow, but apparently had considered, however briefly, putting one of Bertie's brothers on the throne (or so Elizabeth believed). Why would she do such things? One very good reason was that the former Prince of Wales was still very popular among the British people and much of the population romantically believed that he should have been allowed to marry the woman he loved and still be king. Elizabeth had good reason to believe that he might have been reinstated (although he would never have gone back on his word) and she found that she very much liked being Queen. It was not nearly the burden that it was for the monarch—or even later for Prince Philip. She had only to smile and be charming, which came naturally to her. A second reason she wanted the Duke of Windsor exiled (not even a British commoner can be involuntarily exiled—but wait) was that he was the man who had (she believed) publicly spurned her—the man who announced in the newspaper that he had no intention of marrying her. In Windsor's own words, "It was me she wanted to marry." (And, "She's a virulently jealous woman.") In addition, Wallis, an American who felt inferior to nobody (and was not raised in a royal system) was not sufficiently deferential—to Elizabeth or to the private secretaries (Hardinge and Lascelles), whom she saw as glorified servants. The Duke and Duchess of Windsor were history.[5] The Queen Mother saw to it. (The common belief is that she disliked the Windsors because she felt his abdication contributed to her husband's untimely death—by putting him under pressure for which he was unprepared. However, her enmity with the Windsors began long before her husband's death.) She told a friend, in regard to the Windsors, "You think I am a nice person. I am not a nice person."

Some years later her daughter, Princess Margaret, found herself in love with Group Captain Peter Townsend. After heroic efforts during the war, the wounded soldier was assigned as equerry to the King. This was supposed to be a rotating position (to give as many soldiers as possible such an opportunity), but King George VI (Bertie) liked him so much he asked him to stay on. He was a treasure. Whatever the King or the royal family needed to do, he smoothed the way, took care of all the details. He looked after the teenage Princess Margaret. He disapproved of Prince Philip as a husband for Princess Elizabeth (bad move). He was indispensable. He was just never home and so his own marriage disintegrated. At the death of George VI, Elizabeth became Queen and the Queen Mother had to move from Buckingham Palace to Clarence House. Townsend was promoted from Deputy Master of the Royal Household to Comptroller of the Queen Mother's Household.[6] In other words, he was in charge of all the Queen Mother's and Princess Margaret's affairs—domestic, financial, whatever they needed. At this point, having been thrown together continuously for years Princess Margaret and Peter Townsend found themselves very much in love. Princess Margaret asked her sister, the happily married Queen, for permission to marry him. After all was said and done the Queen felt unable to give her permission and Margaret could not marry without it. Publicly Princess Margaret blamed Lascelles (now Private Secretary to the new Queen Elizabeth II). Privately, while she felt her sister could have taken a firmer stand, she knew it was her mother who prevented the marriage—and she never forgave her for ruining her one chance at happiness. The Queen Mother, born commoner, had become more royal than the royals.[7] The thought of her daughter marrying a commoner who was not even titled, who was an equerry (really a glorified servant in her mind), was intolerable. (Remember, the Queen Mother is a good friend and contemporary of Diana's grandmother, Ruth, Lady Fermoy, who testified in court against her own daughter because she wanted her grandchildren to be raised as aristocracy.) The Queen Mother and Margaret left for Rhodesia without him. (Townsend had been scheduled to accompany them, as he always did.) Instead the new Queen took him with her to Belfast, seemingly a step up, but actually simply a move to separate the two lovers. Although Philip had learned of Townsend's disapproval of his own marriage to Elizabeth, his primary concern was for Elizabeth. There must be no scandal to damage the beginning of the young Queen's reign. Before Margaret returned (he had been assured he would be allowed to bid her good-bye) he was shipped off to Brussels without even being given time to see his children and explain to them what was happening. It was to be for two years (watch out for the "two years"), by which time Margaret would be twenty-five and would no longer require her sister's permission to marry—or so she was led to believe at the time. Townsend, another victim of unlawful "involuntary exile," was never to return to England to live.[8] The Queen Mother encouraged the abdication of Edward VIII and made sure his exile was permanent. He, not realizing what was happening, went quietly. The Queen Mother assured Group Captain Peter Townsend was put (and kept) beyond Margaret's reach. Out of respect for Margaret, he, too, went quietly. (A generation later, Sarah, Duchess of York, too, went quietly.)[9]

When Diana and Charles first separated it was generally assumed that after *two years* they would divorce. This is normal procedure in England for uncontested divorces. The plan was for her to be gradually faded from view. It didn't happen. Instead she was becoming more powerful. To make matters worse, she announced to all the world, on her BBC *Panorama* interview, "I won't go quietly"—and thereby signed her own death warrant.

Note: Queen Elizabeth, the Queen Mother, died March 30, 2002, at the age of 102. Her life literally spanned the 20th century. She was a remarkable woman who not only greatly influenced events of the century, but became a symbol of stability during a century that saw more change than any other century in history. At the age of 98, she attended the wedding of her grandson, Prince Edward, to Sophie Rhys-Jones and partied on until 11:00 p.m.

5

THE ROYAL MARRIAGE

Mary, Queen of Scots, the young and beautiful dowager Queen of France, fearing for her life in Scotland, escapes to England and appeals to the Queen for asylum and assistance. The Queen is sympathetic but wary. This young Queen has a claim to the English throne. She may attract followers. Better that she is kept "safe"—guarded, an English prisoner for almost twenty years. Finally there is proof, undeniable proof, of a scheme to take the throne—England's throne—Elizabeth's throne. Although she deplores the action—the Scots Queen is after all a sister monarch, a cousin—she knows her duty. Elizabeth signs the death warrant. It is, after all, for England, for the good of England. It must be done.

    The wedding of the century was letter perfect in every detail, but the marriage it legitimized had some problems. Much of what has been written (and a *lot* has been written) was produced without critical information we now have, so inevitably there were misinterpretations. What we now know is that Charles and Diana had totally different goals and expectations as they entered into what was meant to be a lifetime commitment and partnership. Neither anticipated the media hysteria. Diana was not prepared for the manner in which people's perception of her changed overnight—she was no longer a teenage high school drop-out, she was "the Princess of Wales," future Queen of England, to whom you must curtsy, address as "Ma'am," stop eating when she stops eating. She was no longer a person, but a *personage*. The Prince was unprepared to find the ever-obliging young girl he married change into a wife with ideas and opinions of her own; a young woman who became angry and tearful when he did not provide the attention and support to which she felt she was entitled. She was a romantic (albeit[1] a pragmatic romantic), filled with romance novel plots. In her mind she had built Prince Charles into a bigger than life Prince Charming, someone who could fix all her hurts and fears and make everything wonderful. She wanted—and expected—a full-time husband and lover. He had a full satisfying life before his marriage, without her. What he needed, must have, was someone to provide an heir. If he made any attempt to adapt his life style to accommodate marriage, wife, and children, it didn't show. The one overriding fact—and it is a biggie—is that he was already in a committed relationship. This is the part that is left out of the earlier writings (or at least it is not seen for what it is). Perhaps he truly intended to forsake his soulmate and be true to his wife, but there is little evidence to support this (and certainly Camilla intended the relationship to continue). He continued seeing her throughout the courtship and engagement period even more than he saw Diana, actually spending his wedding eve night with her. (It seems that he really thought he could have both a wife and a mistress. After all, all the men he knew did.) After an overseas tour, it was Camilla he rushed home to—while Diana waited. And Diana knew this, or at least she strongly suspected it, but if she said anything she was immediately branded "paranoid," "jealous," "demanding of attention." In the early years, with youthful optimism, she continued to believe that she could win him away from Camilla. (By all accounts, Charles did break off sexual relations with Camilla for a time, generally considered about two years, but he was in constant contact with her. She was the one he turned to, not Diana. She was even the one he went to with his marital problems—which didn't help them!) Diana tried tears; she tried being seductive. She knew other men found her attractive. Why didn't her husband? She performed the sexy, sensual ballet with Wayne Sleep in a final desperate attempt to seduce her husband. Instead of being attracted by her charms, Charles was embarrassed that she would "make a spectacle of herself." (This is the same man who, on his wedding day, looked at his mother for permission to kiss his bride.)

The leap from commoner to royal is a much greater leap than is generally realized, and goes a long way in explaining the extreme stress the Princess was feeling. Americans generally tend to equate British royalty with American Hollywood. Really there is no comparison. Except for the money and publicity, both of which may be short term, Hollywood stars are not that different from the rest of us. (How many Hollywood stars have servants who must back out of their presence?) Royalty, on the other hand, are simply a different breed. For all their wealth and privilege nothing is ever simple for them. Because they were born to the wealth and privilege, they take it for granted until it is taken away from them. This rarely happens. When the former King Edward VIII left England, following his abdication, he was surprised to discover that someone was not always there to automatically smooth the way. Someone had always taken care of all his needs. He had made almost no practical plans for his life after abdication. Someone had to tell him that he needed to make a hotel reservation in Paris. They are set apart.

Andrew Morton relates a revealing story. Sitting at her desk in the Palace one winter day, the Queen noticed the ducks shivering near the frozen pond and decided to feed them—a simple enough gesture for most people, even a Hollywood star. For the Queen, however, at least half a dozen people were involved. First she must summon her Page of the Back Stairs, who, after finding out what the Queen wants, passes the message to the Number Two footman, who telephones the Chef. While the kitchen staff prepare the bread crumbs, another footman makes the half-mile round trip to the kitchens to pick up the package. Meanwhile, the Queen's dresser lays out her favorite overcoat, galoshes, scarf and gloves. The Queen's page collects her corgis, then delivers the package of bread crumbs on a silver tray. Finally, the Queen can go feed the ducks. Even for Diana, a simple "private" day such as lunch with friends involved a security check in advance, an ambulance on standby, police surveillance, her dresser making sure her outfit was ready, a detective to accompany her. A "work" day or formal occasion required much, much more. Protocol must always be followed; the chain of command must be followed exactly.

In the beginning if Prince Philip wanted a late night snack he was expected to go through the same convoluted procedure. This did not last long. If he wanted a snack he simply contacted the kitchen staff. (Later he had kitchenettes installed in the royal apartments.) When Diana first moved into Buckingham Palace she frequently visited the kitchens because she felt more at ease there. She had to be told that she was not supposed to be there. (On her honeymoon cruise, she spent more time with the crew than with her bride groom, who was either reading or getting a suntan.) She was no longer "Diana," much less "Duch;" she was either "Your Royal Highness" or "Ma'am." Add to this the unprecedented pressure of the media. Never before in history has anyone been so constantly followed and intruded upon by the paparazzi as Charles and Diana—and the major thrust was on the unsuspecting and unprepared Diana. With all the glut of photographs, relatively few of them are of the Prince alone. Some exceptions include his visit to the hospital at the time of William's birth and some photos of him with the children—sometimes for the purpose of improving his image; especially after Prince William's head injury, when he was perceived as not being concerned enough. It was not always so. During the Margaret-Townsend affair, the Palace was able to persuade the media to keep the affair quiet. When King Edward VIII was preparing to abdicate the whole world knew about it before the British people knew about it. The Palace is no longer able to maintain this control. Never before has royalty—or anyone else—been exposed to the unrelenting, unforgiving media coverage of the last few decades. No other royal couple has had to live their life under such "fish bowl" conditions. When King Edward VIII made his abdication speech in 1936 because he felt he could not rule "without the help and support of the woman I love," it was broadcast on the radio and heard in hundreds, perhaps thousands, of homes. (Prior to the abdication, almost right up until it happened, the British press kept quiet as a result of "a gentlemen's agreement." While stories and pictures of the Prince of Wales and Wallis Simpson were appearing in newspapers all over the world, the British people were kept in the dark.) A new era had begun. Maintaining their privacy and the illusion that royals are somehow different, that they are not afflicted with the trials and tribulations of commoners, would become more and more difficult for the royals. The coronation of King George VI and Queen Elizabeth (the Queen Mother) was also broadcast, a program lasting seven hours (but not the actual ceremony), on 300 American stations, said to be the longest continuous program in American radio history at that time. When the Queen was crowned in 1953 she insisted, against the advice of her counselors, that the event be televised. She clearly understood the value of her vast and diverse family of subjects actually seeing her crowned—and, as always, she was right. ("I must be seen to be believed," she said.) But it was a two-edged sword—the more the public saw and heard, the more they wanted to see and hear. The lid was off Pandora's box. Yet not until the wedding of Charles and Diana did "royal watching" become an international obsession. For the first ten years of the marriage the face of the Princess seemed to be on every magazine cover—and sales zoomed when it was. The Queen did what she could to protect her, but the Palace no longer has this control. They can't even control what the servants tell; the media pays better. However, when I toured Kensington Palace in 1986 as an ordinary tourist, I talked with one of the women working there. She was eager to know what was happening with Charles and Diana. "We don't hear anything," she said.

During Diana's first pregnancy the Queen herself asked them to give her some space. They were polite, but continued their constant vigilance, printing anything and everything, including the now famous bikini shot when she was five months pregnant. She was too marketable. The Queen is photographed in public and when she is prepared. Part of this has to do with a difference in their life styles. Diana continued to try to live a somewhat "normal" life, doing her own shopping, going out for lunch with friends. This, the media felt, made her fair game. However, there is another factor. The obsession with Diana was not due to her being royal (the Queen is as royal as they come); but was due to her being a "Cinderella" who found her Prince Charming. It was an expression of an overwhelming psychological need of people, especially women, to believe in a real fairy tale—a fairy tale with a happy ending. It was the Soap Opera Supreme, the Perfect Movie.

In working with stress, and stressors, certain life events have been found to be especially powerful. These include such things as the death of a loved one, marriage, divorce, new baby, change of job, major move (as across country—or into a palace), among others. Looking at this list it is easy to see that Diana was exposed to a tremendous amount of stress. Marriage, becoming a royal, becoming a mother, being a working mother, all at a very young age and in a very short time. Add to this the constant recording and reporting of her every word and action. (In addition to the media, for her own protection she was constantly monitored and accompanied—*all* the time, not just on tours, not just on state occasions, but 24 hours a day, seven days a week.) Add to the burden that she is trying very hard to be an asset to her husband and to the Queen, fearful that she will in some way embarrass them, and, although she is doing a wonderful job, nobody tells her so because that is not the way of royals. She is simply doing what is expected, what they are used to and have done all their lives, and so they don't know to praise and encourage her. Yet she lacks confidence and self-esteem and badly needs their reassurance. (Some have said or implied that she was very confident and "scheming." If this were true she would not have suffered bulimia—only those who feel totally overwhelmed become bulimic, and her fingernails would not have been chewed to the quick.) She might have "schemed" to get her man as many a young woman has done, but not in the sense that she was being devious or underhanded. She had no way of knowing how relentless the pressure would be—and how little support she would have. Unfortunately, she always looked wonderful, so it was hard for people to really understand the turmoil she was experiencing. She was afraid to appear in public without her husband, yet when they were together she stole the show and he did not like it. In the early years she was either unable to speak in public or was not allowed to. There were other hurdles. Not only was Charles almost thirteen years older than Diana, but they were almost of different generations. He liked classical music (so did she, and she was a fairly accomplished pianist—her grandmother gave up a career as a concert pianist to marry), she liked pop; he liked the country life, she preferred the metropolitan; he liked cold, damp Scotland (she loved Scotland, too, just not Balmoral where she felt overwhelmed), she preferred the sunny Caribbean. His friends were all older and also had different interests. Except for their children and "the job," they had very little in common.

Charles, meanwhile, was having his own problems. He knew how to be royal. The problem was that he had always been the star. At first he was proud of Diana and enjoyed showing her off, but almost from the beginning (their first visit to Wales) the crowd made it clear that they wanted Diana, not Charles. This was hard on his ego. He, too, had worked all his life for praise and approval and, while he had had it from the public, he had had very little from his father. Consider, too, that Charles really did not want to marry. He was happy the way he was. He had everything he needed. Marriage was a *duty* for him. It was part of his job to provide an heir and to do that he must needs marry a healthy young Protestant woman of good breeding. He did exactly that, but since he has always been the center of attention, totally catered to, he did not know how to communicate, how to compromise. (His brother Andrew ran into the same problem.) Diana must have felt at times that she was a breeding animal, nothing more. This was surely reinforced after Charles told the whole world that he never loved her. However she felt about Charles at that time, hearing this publicly stated must have been extremely humiliating. In addition, any feelings of rejection caused all her childhood fears and pain to break through, making the emotion much more intense than it might otherwise have been. (In contrast, the Queen had an incredibly protected and sheltered childhood, developing an absolute sense of security. When she learned of Philip's unfaithfulness she had a very difficult time with it, but there were no painful childhood memories associated with it.)

In the beginning Diana was still very much in awe of her husband, the Prince of Wales, afraid to talk back, and "terrified" of the Queen, to whom she always gave a full royal greeting—curtsy and kiss on each cheek. Gradually, the overwhelming response of the people to her everywhere she went gave her some confidence that she was doing something right, so gradually she began to talk back to him. He was not used to this. Nobody *ever* talked back to him, so the talks very quickly escalated into shouting matches. (One girlfriend, Anna Wallace, did talk back, but then she was not his girl friend any more.) There was little real communication. For years, the confusion resulting from the almost hysterical adoration of the public juxtaposed against the criticism or silence of her husband and the rest of the royal family was overwhelming. One minute she was a megastar; the next she was being dressed down for having said or done something that "isn't done." Since she still judged herself by what others seemed to think of her, she was constantly up and down, totally unsure of who she was. It seems she was always told what not to do after the fact. It left her afraid to trust her own judgment. Actually, she had always been afraid to trust her own judgment. This just confirmed it. Her clothes reflect her turmoil (more on this later). Add to that roller coaster her physiological mood swings resulting from the bulimia and it is easy to see why conflicting reports were written.

In his own way Charles tried to help her at first. He guided her through basic protocol. When her stress level became untenable he called in his friend and mentor Sir Laurens Van der Post, who immediately recognized her need for psychiatric help. What Charles did *not* do was adjust his life style to accommodate his marriage. He went on exactly as he always had, including spending time with Camilla, expecting Diana to somehow fit in.

Much has been written about Diana's bulimia—especially how it has its roots in dysfunctional families and is triggered by stress. This tends to take the blame off Charles. But there is another factor. (This is true of most psychological problems—the key is in the language we use.) She was forced to "swallow" so much, especially the knowledge of Charles's continued liaison with Camilla, but also her constant fear of making a public mistake (remember, this is the child who believes she will not be kept if she is not good enough—the child who would only take non-speaking parts in school plays) that it simply has to "come back up" or she will choke to death.

She had a terrific amount of responsibility for one so young and she was a perfectionist.[2] Some have commented on the amount of control Charles allowed her. Actually, it was more a case of, "You handle it." He did not want to be bothered with it. Owning homes, having babies—he was not used to any of it and, while he liked parts of it, he did not let it interfere with his life—nor did he give up his comforter.

At first Charles was proud of his well-received bride, feeling he was the "producer," but as the crowds continued to want *her* he was, to put it bluntly, jealous. It hurt his feelings. He had worked hard all his life to be accepted, to be taken seriously, and suddenly all anybody was interested in was what his wife was wearing. He had never played second fiddle and he did not plan to start now.

It is difficult for us mere mortals to imagine the complexity of a life where everything must go through the appropriate channels and servants sometimes seem to have more power than their masters. When Charles decided to ask Diana to the opera, followed by supper in his apartments (their first public "date") he wrote the following memo to his valet, Stephen Barry, "Please ring Captain Anthony Asquith before going out shooting and tell him that I have asked Lady Diana Spencer (Lady Fermoy's granddaughter) to come to the Albert Hall and dinner afterwards at BP on Sunday evening. Please ask if this can be arranged and she will arrive with her grandmother at the Albert Hall. If it is all right, please ask him to ring back at lunchtime when we will be at the House {Buckingham Palace}. C." Can you imagine they might have said they could not arrange it, sorry? When Diana went to lunch with friends—a simple private occasion, it involved her dresser, her hairdresser, her detective, her chauffeur, her private secretary—perhaps others. An ambulance with driver was on standby nearby, the restaurant was checked out in advance. Scotland Yard monitored her every move. That is just for a simple, private lunch. Imagine what was involved for a public occasion or a state dinner. Overseas tours were like military campaigns.

The media were always a part of the marriage, starting well before even the engagement, especially of Diana's activities. In many pictures, the hundreds of flashing bulbs can be seen, but it was not the numbers, it was the constancy, the never-stoppingness.

The first few months following the birth of William was a good period. The Prince and Princess of Wales doted on their new baby and spent hours in the nursery playing with him, bathing him, behaving like any other new parents. No other royal baby ever had such hands-on parenting—and by both parents. It was a time of sharing, of contentment, but there was also postnatal depression to deal with, especially bad because of all the unresolved issues. Then came Remembrance Day in November, less than five months after William's birth. This is an important event, and was especially important in this year of the Falklands conflict. The unthinkable happened. Diana arrived *after* the Queen. Of all the things that "aren't done," this is just absolutely at the top of the list. *Nobody* arrives after the Queen. Diana did. Much has been written about what might or might not have happened. I can easily imagine. Look at her picture. It's the one in the blue and black silk dress with the black tie belt. This is her first public appearance since the birth of her baby. She looks—with the help of the wind, which she called "her enemy"—like a sausage tied in the middle. It is, without doubt, one of the most unflattering pictures ever published of her. I can imagine her dressing for her postnatal debut and discovering that nothing fits, becoming so distressed that she can't go, but then realizing that she *must* go and—as she so often has—she put on her public face and forced herself to go. It went well enough. She was reported to be "radiant and happy" by the end of the evening. But, then, she would have seen the pictures the next day. It was at this point that she determined to lose weight. Whatever method she chose was obviously successful. Soon photos were of a much slimmer Princess, but it took its toll on her emotional health and undoubtedly exacerbated her bulimia. Since bulimia depletes the system of essential nutrients, causing serious mood swings, not until late in her second pregnancy was she was able to re-establish her equilibrium. (According to Diana, their marriage was at its best and most stable during this second pregnancy.) That ended the day Prince Harry was born and his father welcomed him into the world with, "Oh, God, it's a boy—and he's even got red hair." As Diana herself said, "Something inside me closed off." (He was hoping for a girl. Diana had known for some time that she was carrying another son, but had kept it to herself. The red hair was a Spencer trait—yet Diana also noted that over the years, he was "very close" to Harry.) The marriage was essentially over at that point.

If clothes make the man, they tell a story about the woman who wears them. Diana has often compared herself to Eliza Dolittle of "My Fair Lady." The concept in this play was that by changing the language of the Cockney Miss you could actually change the person. Clothing works in a similar way. A study of Diana's wardrobe over the last fifteen years tells her story in vivid visual detail from the early pre-royal Sloane Ranger outfits to her final royal chic. Her way of dressing was one of the first things Charles noticed about the sixteen year old girl. "I like seeing a lady well dressed. It was one of the things I always noticed about her before we were married. She had, I thought, a very good sense of style and design."

A comparison of three of the most photographed women in the world—and their clothes—Diana, Princess of Wales; Queen Elizabeth II and Jacqueline Kennedy, American First Lady, is revealing.

These three women have several things in common. All three came into their public role at a young age, newly married, with young children, and with husbands who were sometimes difficult. Of the three only the Queen was trained for the role from childhood and even she, normally, would have had much more time before being thrust into the limelight (It was Jackie who said, "It is frightening to lose one's anonymity at such a young age.") All three were nervous in the sense that they lacked experience and they very much did not want to make mistakes, certainly not in public. If it sometimes seems that there is too much emphasis on clothes it is precisely because this is how we, the public, "know" these glamorous personalities; it is how we know these women whose roles are powerful but largely symbolic. Consciously or unconsciously, people's personalities are reflected in their clothing styles. The Queen and Jackie are of the same generation—the hat and gloves generation. However, Jackie often appeared to be barelegged. For church, she frequently substituted a scarf or lace mantilla for the required head covering. Her holidays were spent on beaches and in sunny climes while the Queen preferred cold and damp Balmoral in Scotland. Born in the 'Sixties, Diana was of a less formal generation. "Dressing for the job" is a full-time task. Both the Queen and Diana have/had "dressers," whose sole job is to care for their clothes and accessories, lay them out each day, assist with fittings and pack them carefully for overseas tours. Jackie had maids with similar responsibilities.

The Queen has been described as "dowdy" or "frumpy," but nobody has ever accused her of not being regal. She may appear careless of her wardrobe, less glamorous than her sister Margaret. Careless she is not. Her clothes, like Diana's, are "for the job" and must be comfortable and suitable to whatever climate she finds herself in. The Queen is never careless about anything, least of all her appearances in public. She never wears the same outfit twice in public, feeling that "the people" have a right to see their Queen in something nobody else has yet seen. The outfits themselves are perfect to the last detail, but they are also non-threatening to women, unobtrusive to men and highly visible to the crowds—and they are thoroughly British. Too chic would suggest French; too youthful American. (However, she is probably happiest in her "casual" clothes or overcoat and Wellingtons, watching her horses.) The richest, most powerful woman in the world maintains her power partly by her ability to allow middle-class commoners to identify with her. Like her mother, the Queen Mother, she is a genius at this. Having grown up during World War II and come of age in an extremely economically depressed England, she was thrilled with her magnificent trousseau, comprised partly of gifts and partly of additional clothing coupons provided by the government. But she had work to do. She had to maintain the gains her father had made during his relatively short reign. She had her mother's example and resources. She quickly set up a system with the royal couturier, Norman Hartnell, that provided the excellence that was her standard with a minimum of her time and effort. Her hair was done weekly, but she had fittings almost daily. The Queen knows exactly who she is—and ever has.

Jackie grew up quite differently from the Queen, but she, too, was familiar with the world of designers. Jackie, looking at a four to eight year reign rather than a life-time (only three years as it turned out) selected one couturier, Oleg Cassini, to create a look unique to her. (It was his idea, but she was smart enough to see the advantages.) He did just that. It was a look of understated elegance and suited her perfectly. It never changed. It also hid her perfectly. Her clothing not only concealed her moods and feelings, they actually concealed her pregnancy except in the final months. Her outfits were always dazzling, but rarely surprising. Bateau neckline, sleeveless or cap sleeves, A-line skirt in many different fabrics and combinations, often with a "signature" bow, describes most of her lovely designer outfits. She put American fashion on the map, as Diana later did British fashion. She knew how she wanted to be perceived. (A heavy smoker, she was rarely photographed with a cigarette.) The Queen was twenty-five when she became Queen. Jacqueline Kennedy was thirty when she became First Lady. Diana was nineteen when she became engaged to the Prince of Wales. How could she possibly know her "look"? She did not even know who she was. Number-wise, this is not much difference, but at this stage in life there is considerable difference. Diana was still a teenager—she probably had never worn a hat; the Queen and Jackie were young women, young mothers. In the beginning Diana's youthfulness showed in the frilly details of her outfits—ruffles, bows, ribbons, embroidery. At first, she used a wide variety of designers, unsure of the look she wanted, trying to meet everybody's expectations, reacting to good or bad media coverage. Gradually she narrowed her choice of designers, but, unlike the Queen, she continued to use a wide variety. (This was partly to provide patronage to as many as possible, knowing that her patronage would practically guarantee their success.) The Emanuels were dropped early because they were not discreet enough; Catherine Walker, Bruce Oldfield and Victor Edelstein remained favorites. Belville Sassoon, Jasper Conran and Jan Van Velden were also much in evidence. She bought "off the peg" if it suited her. John Boyd, Philip Somerville and Frederick Fox did her wonderful hats. (My favorite, a gray and white straw, was done by Marina Killery.) Gradually, a much more elegant, streamlined look emerged, along with a shorter, sleeker hairstyle to accentuate it. Diana, particularly, made it a point to honor the place or group she was visiting by wearing something appropriate (all red, white and blue on her first visit for the United States, for example; the Welsh colors of red and green for her first visit to Wales). Of the three, Diana is the only one whose pregnancies were so public. The Queen's first two children were born before she was queen and before the media became so aggressive; she stayed out of the public eye during her last two pregnancies. Jackie's two children were born before her husband became president. She did have one pregnancy while he was in office, but spent the summer mostly in Hyanisport prior to Patrick's premature birth and short life. Diana, on the other hand, worked and was photographed throughout her two pregnancies right up until delivery time. (This also reflects a change in society regarding pregnant women. In the first half of the century women who were visibly pregnant were expected to either stay out of sight or, if they must be seen, to camouflage the pregnancy in some way.) After her separation and divorce, Diana began to wear all the things she could not wear before. She turned to more daring designers such as Jacques Azagury. She had used him before, but now she allowed him to do the more daring outfits. And Catherine Walker's designs became sleeker and sexier. There was a sense of the sixteen year old defying parental authority by wearing her skirts too tight and too short; heels too high. Sixteen years of wearing flats had to be compensated for. She no longer had to dress "for the job," but could finally dress like the modern young woman she was. Still it was reassuring to see her clothes eventually become more serene, not demure, but with sleeker lines, vee necklines instead of the high necked blouses she wore in the early years. There was a serenity, a sense of who she was, about her clothes that was not evident before. She also favored some foreign designers such as Valentino and Versace, but was ever mindful of her responsibility to the British clothing industry.

Jewelry—or is jewellery? No story about royal clothing can be complete without the mention of jewelry. Jackie wore very little jewelry, perhaps because she did not own fabulous heirloom pieces such as her guests or hosts often wore. Better not compete if you are always going to come out second best. Jackie was not a second-best person. She usually wore a three strand pearl necklace, often mostly hidden inside her dress. (We know now that not even the pearls were real.) Apparently, it was not until she married Aristotle Onassis that she had very much real jewelry. She sometimes wore an antique sunburst hairpiece that almost had the look of a tiara.

The Queen has one of the most fabulous jewel collections in the world. For state affairs or when she feels the need to impress others, she wears her fabulous collections—sapphires, diamonds, rubies, emeralds—with her formal attire. (The gems are so large they don't look real.) For daytime outfits, however, in spite of all the pieces she has to choose from, she almost always wears a pearl necklace, usually three strands, with Queen Mary's Devon pearl and diamond earrings (a wedding gift) or some other pearl earrings. The only thing that varies is the brooch that she wears on the left side. (A memorable rare occasion: for the wedding of the Duke and Duchess of York she was persuaded to turn the diamond clasp of her pearls to one side and omit the brooch. For the wedding of the Prince and Princess of Wales she wore the magnificent pink diamond flower brooch.)[3] This is probably another example of perfection with minimum time and effort. You can hardly go wrong with a perfectly matched set of pearls.

Prince Philip has designed several pieces of jewelry for the Queen, including her engagement ring and a wedding gift bracelet—made from his mother's tiara. One of her favorite brooches is his naval insignia set in diamonds, which he also designed and presented as a wedding gift.

No discussion of royal jewelry would be complete without mention of the Queen's Family Order. These are presented by the monarch to family members in recognition of their service to the crown. They are simply jeweled portraits of the monarch on a ribbon. The Queen herself wears two (one with her father's portrait and one with her grandfather's portrait). The Queen's is on a yellow ribbon. (Several of Diana's formal dresses were designed to complement it, for instance, the yellow taffeta ball gown first worn in Australia in 1983.)

Diana came into the public eye with almost no jewelry (*jewellery*, if you are British) of her own, but wedding gifts (including some from the Queen) soon remedied that. In addition, she continued to receive jewelry from Charles, from heads of state and from wealthy friends. She had fun jewelry as well as the "real stuff." In addition, many of her pieces have sentimental value. For example, in most of her early daytime photos, she is wearing a charm bracelet with a koala bear charm, a gift from the Prince. She also frequently wore the diamond heart that he gave her at the birth of William, as well as a gold disk on which William's handwritten name is engraved. (One of the issues that had to be settled during the divorce negotiations was which gifts belong to her personally and which are only hers in trust. This was not a major problem since her jewels would logically go to her son anyway. Certainly it is not the problem that it was when the Duchess of Windsor ended up with many royal jewels—and, of course, for Diana it turned out not to be a problem at all.) The Queen herself did not have many jewels prior to her marriage, although she could always borrow from her mother. As an infant she was given her mother's coral bead necklace and her father followed Queen Victoria's example of giving each of his daughter's two pearls on each birthday, eventually forming a complete necklace. Her grandfather, King George V, gave the Princesses Elizabeth and Margaret each a pearl necklace (two strands for Margaret; three for Elizabeth) to mark his silver jubilee. The Princesses wore these at the coronation of their parents in 1937. For birthdays she received brooches or bracelets, not only from her parents, but also from her grandmother, Queen Mary. She received her "first diamonds" (a long strand, later divided to form a necklace and matching bracelet) from the South African Government for her twenty-first birthday, shortly before her engagement to Prince Philip was announced. Although, the Queen has sometimes had certain pieces dismantled and redesigned, it was Diana who was wondrously imaginative with her jewelry. She made her jewelry fun—as she did her clothes. In addition to using "paste" jewelry when it suited her—or her outfit—she has transformed Queen Mary's art deco diamond and emerald choker into a headband. She has tied a rope of "pearls" down her bare back (not fun to sit on, she reported), or worn a bow tie in lieu of diamonds.

By studying their clothes, we can know (or not know) the women. The Queen is traditional perfection. She knows who she is. Jackie hid behind understated elegance. She knew how she wanted to be perceived. Diana floundered, but struggled to find herself and was not afraid to express her mood. We, her public, were allowed to observe her evolution from insecure teenage fiancée to poised Princess of Wales; from the joy of her first pregnancy to the breakdown of her marriage to the finding of her true self. Any number of magazines and books have used Diana's fashion styles to show how she has evolved over the years, but even more interesting has been the look at the *day to day* changes. This is where you can see her uncertainty, her switching back and forth according to what the media are saying. Gradually, her own style became apparent, independent of the opinions of others.[4] As Diana found her style, as she came to know herself and believe in herself, she found it more and more difficult to stay in a marriage that was no marriage. Previous royal wives were expected to do this, and did. Born in the 'Sixties, Diana was a modern woman. This kind of hypocrisy was contrary to her nature and unacceptable in today's feminist society. It also left her in a very untenable position. She could not have a discreet lover as others might have had because the media dogged her every move. (They seemingly were not interested in what Charles was doing, or with whom.) It also left her lonely and alone when she was at the height of her sexuality. What was she to do? She also felt very threatened by the "courtiers" and by the Prince's "people." (She never publicly blamed Charles, himself, but always "his office" or "his people"—and often referred to them as "the enemy.") They were determined that the Prince look good to the public and the best way to accomplish that was to make Diana look bad. She made the trip to South Korea as she had promised the Queen, but by now, aware of Charles's efforts to disgrace her, it was impossible to continue to look like a happy couple even to please the people and to keep her promise to the Queen. By now even the Queen recognized that the marriage was over and it was time to acknowledge it.

6

END OF THE FAIRY TALE

"I can not rule without the help and support of the woman I love." The King is explaining to the people why he must abdicate the throne of England to his brother Bertie. It is in England's best interest. It must be done. He has been told that he must choose between the throne and the woman he loves. He has chosen the woman. Bertie is now King George VI, King of England. Edward VIII, now Duke of Windsor, is not allowed to marry his love on English soil, nor is he ever allowed to return to England to live. Born to be King, having committed no crime, he is effectively and forever exiled from his native land. He dies in Paris in the house Diana and Dodi toured on August 31, 1997, the day Diana died.

On December 9, 1992, at the end of the six months moratorium set by the Queen, Prime Minister John Major read the following statement in the House of Commons:

"It is announced from Buckingham Palace that with regret the Prince and Princess of Wales have decided to separate. Their Royal Highnesses have no plans to divorce and their constitutional positions are unaffected.

"This decision has been reached amicably…The Queen and Duke of Edinburgh, though saddened, understand and sympathize with the difficulties which have led to this decision…"

Most of the points made in the announcement could be argued, but for the time being, Charles moved his things out of Kensington Palace and Diana moved her things out of Highgrove. Both parents were still very much involved with the young Princes and were sometimes together for special occasions such as the 50th Anniversary of VE Day celebrations or William's entrance into Eton.

Polls sprang up like mushrooms—by some counts as many as fifty per cent of the citizens now believed the end of the monarchy was in sight. Members of Parliament debated Charles's right to be King. Charles was concerned enough to seek legal advice from one of the best in the field. He was reassured that a divorced King could reign—but a remarried one might not. Charles immediately announced that he would not remarry—and he would be King. (The implication was that he would be celibate.)

Labor MP Anthony Benn introduced a bill to abolish the monarchy. It was never debated—but neither was he charged with treason.

A "close personal friend to the Queen Mother" (when the royals wish to make public comments they do it through a trusted media person) chose the *Sunday Times* to transmit the Queen Mother's message: "Princess Diana could never have won a university place, but she won a prince and failed to keep him She is addicted to the limelight her marriage brought. It's like a drug; to feed her craving she will do anything, even if it meant (sic) destroying the throne she solemnly swore to uphold." [When did she swear to uphold the throne? She had been married, not crowned.] The Queen Mother could have been describing herself. Academics and intellectuality have never been high priorities for the royals. The Queen was tutored at home and poorly prepared for her position. The Queen's grandfather was so unlearned that his son, the Duke of Windsor, backed out on a planned biography because he didn't want the world to know how poorly educated his father, King George V, was. Charles is the first heir to the throne to earn a degree, although others, including the Duke of Windsor, did attend University. Only with Diana did it become an issue. It could also be argued that she never really "won a prince," only the title. (Much has been made of the fact that both Diana and Fergie were products of broken homes—the Queen Mother, herself non-royal, does not support the theory that their non-royal status is the problem. Everyone seems to have forgotten that the Queen herself chose a partner whose parents were divorced—and this was when divorce was really rare, almost unheard of among royals.)

Much has been written and said about Diana's alleged manipulation of the media. This is not necessarily good or bad. As Diana herself said, "If they are always going to be there why not make use of them?" What most people don't know—or at least those who knew are long since gone on to their reward—is how the Queen Mother manipulated the press—right from the beginning. Apparently no one knows how the news item concerning her imminent engagement to the Prince of Wales happened to be printed. What is known is that, as soon as her engagement to Bertie was announced on January 15, 1923, she held her own press conference. Absolutely unheard of! She was, of course, scolded by the Palace (wonderful term, that—it carries ultimate authority and leaves no one responsible or accountable). No matter. She had already accomplished her goal. The press were now totally and devotedly on her side, where they remained throughout the century.

In any crisis the Queen Mother took to her bed until it was over. One exception—when her daughter, Princess Margaret, had to make the most difficult decision of her life, the choice between love and duty, she was well enough; but she had retired to her Castle Mey in Scotland—well out of the line of fire.

Warned by friends that there was a conspiracy against her, Diana desperately looked for a way out, a way to protect herself, to keep her children. She decided to trust royal writer Andrew Morton to tell "her true story," believing that the people would support her if they only knew the real situation; but also knowing that she would never be forgiven by the royal family. At this point she was desperate. She then let certain friends know that she would not object if they talked to Morton. After her death we learned that, according to Morton, she herself was interviewed for the book, although it was done through a third party so that she could honestly say that she had never met Morton.

The book told of her bulimia, her husband's lack of warmth and affection, and hinted strongly of his affair with Camilla. It appeared June 15, 1992. From that moment there was no chance of reconciliation. Charles was outraged. Even Diana was dismayed by the extent of detail. The Palace demanded a statement from Diana that the book had been written without her knowledge or consent. At first she attempted to distance herself from the book, but then, with her friends' reputations on the line, she made it clear that they were still her friends. The message to the palace was clear, but the Queen was not unaware of the hold the Princess had over the people and insisted on a "show of unity." So she was with the royal family for Royal Ascot. Snubbed by Prince Philip, Diana was cheered by the crowds. The Queen called a crisis meeting. She insisted on a six months "cooling off" period, during which time they would continue to present a united front and would make their scheduled trip to South Korea. Diana agreed. "I know my duty," she told the Queen. But then Charles and his friends developed a "four-point plan." First there would be a public relations campaign to improve the Prince's image, emphasizing his commitment to his work, the country, and the environment. Secondly, his friends would let it be known that they were sympathetic to the Prince, but he did not want them to say anything. Third, they would anonymously leak "his side." Finally and most importantly, they would explain that the marital problems were all Diana's fault, but due to her unbalanced emotional state she could not be held accountable. That seemed to cover all the bases. It began with "The Case for Charles" in the *Sunday Times*. Penny Junor assured the people that Camilla and Charles were just "very good friends," and "if Diana would agree to treatment, Charles would give it another try." (Remember, Diana has been in treatment since the early months of the marriage.)

Then something strange happened. First a taped conversation between Diana and James Gilbey was released, making Diana look very bad indeed[1]—although supporters quickly pointed out that she was a very lonely woman, what was she to do? Shortly thereafter a taped conversation between Charles and Camilla was released—an extremely intimate and private conversation (as Diana's was; however, with Charles and Camilla there was obviously more than just talk).[2] Both of these conversations were obtained illegally, but what was strange was that both conversations were recorded at the end of 1989—Diana's on New Year's Eve (when she was obviously alone) and Charles and Camilla a few days earlier. Why were they released *three years* after they occurred? Why were *both* Charles and Diana being embarrassed? Is it the monarchy itself someone is trying to undermine? There were suggestions of conspiracies, perhaps by the British MI5 (British Intelligence Service)—To embarrass the royal family? To undermine the monarchy? Why? (Dale, Lady Tryon, confidante of the Prince—who also died very unexpectedly—believed there was a conspiracy. She was quoted as saying, "What I suggest is that people stop and think deeper about all these so-called revelations. I believe the republican groups are trying to undermine the country and bring the monarchy down. I suggest the people and the press are being maneuvered by somebody to bring about the monarchy's destruction.")

Shortly after the separation of the Prince and Princess and the release of the Camillagate tape, in May of 1993, a conversation (in their home, not on a phone) between Charles and Diana was released.

Meanwhile, Diana continued her work with the hospitals, the hospices, the ill and the bereaved. The public adored Diana and saw her as a woman who had been badly wronged. While the Palace appeared to support her (they had to with public opinion so strong), behind the scenes they sabotaged her. They kept her from becoming president of the British Red Cross; when she was invited to present the prestigious Richard Dimbleby Lecture regarding her views on AIDS, she was stopped; when she asked to go to Saudi Arabia she was told that it was too dangerous (she and Princess Anne were going together), Prince Charles should go to Saudi Arabia and she could go to Germany to comfort the families of the soldiers. When she wanted to go to Northern Ireland to comfort the grieving parents of two children killed by IRA bombs, Prince Philip was sent instead.

By December of 1993 Diana felt defeated. She stood before a group of 500 gathered at the Park Lane Hilton, London, and with a voice near tears, explained that she would be "retiring from public life" in order to give more time to her children, "who need and deserve as much love, care, and attention as I can give them...I hope you can find it in your hearts to understand and to give me time and space that has been sadly lacking in recent years..." (Penny Thornton, astrologer to the Princess, feels that this was not, in fact, Diana's decision at all, but that "she was made to do this.")

At this point, on the recommendation of the Prime Minister, the Queen wrote letters to Diana and Charles directing them to divorce "sooner than later" for the sake of the boys. Then she made sure the public was made aware of her action. Although Charles responded immediately as she requested, Diana felt she needed time to think about it and discuss it with her lawyers. Finally, two months later, at the end of February—and after considerable nudging by the Queen's Private Secretary, Diana agreed to meet with Charles to discuss a divorce. She insisted that no one else be there—no lawyers, no secretaries, no courtiers. She agreed to the divorce provided Charles made it clear that *he* was the one requesting it. She was determined not to be seen as a "bolter," like her mother. He was the one who asked her to marry him; he must be the one to ask to end it. She then called the Queen, admitting that it was "the saddest day" of her life.

Negotiations were lengthy and detailed, but eventually Diana was awarded a lump sum of $26,000,000.00,[3] to be awarded over a period of five years, plus an additional $660,000.00 annually for office and staff expenses. She was allowed to remain in Kensington Palace until she chose to move or she married. The jewels were hers for life,[4] after which they would go to Prince William for his bride. (There were stipulations. She could not sell or lend any jewels given to her by members of the royal family. Fair enough.) Of course, the couple would share custody of the children. She was not allowed to keep her royal title of *Her Royal Highness*, but this was largely because of Prince Philip and the Queen Mother. On her own the Queen probably would have allowed it. (Diana pushed her luck when she suggested Clarence House as a London home "after the death of the Queen Mother." Nobody wanted to be reminded that even the Queen Mum could not live forever.) Although Prince Charles wanted her stripped of all perks, the Queen did not agree. She was still allowed to use the Queen's Flight, provided she was traveling with her children, and would, so they said, still be considered a part of the royal family on certain occasions. (Some said when pigs fly.)

Would Diana really have married Dodi? Of course not. She was simply getting back at the British Establishment and having a little fun in the process. She was also getting back at Charles who was getting ready to go public with Camilla. She told friends that, while she was having a wonderful time, she was not ready to go into another marriage. She would have recognized the problem of a stepfather for William who was unacceptable to the Establishment. She would have been concerned about his history of irresponsibility and womanizing. She was always first and foremost concerned about her children, and especially William, as future king. She might have been tempted. She had an almost pathological need for the affection and attention he was giving her (daddy's orders?). He was rich with a capital R (at least his father was). Like Jackie Kennedy, she might have perceived his wealth as protection from the Establishment and the media. Some have suggested that she saw in him the same things that caused her to fall in love with Charles. He lost his mother at an early age, grew up in boarding schools. His father remarried a younger woman and had another family, so Dodi, like Charles and like Diana, grew up feeling lonely, without a mother's presence, with the sadness of their losses.

Diana had a history of making bad choices where men were concerned—Charles who rejected her; James Hewett who betrayed her; and James Gilbey who left her. Because of her childhood traumas from her parents' stormy marriage and her perceived abandonment, a good relationship was probably not in the cards for her. I am sure, however, that in the final analysis she would have put William's needs first and rejected marriage with the son of Mohammed al Fayed, if she had, indeed, ever really considered it.

Diana looked different that last year. I have studied and studied her pictures. I know she had a new hairstyle, updated make-up; still there was something more. Finally I realized what it was. She *knew.* She knew that her time had run out and she had finally accepted it. (Diana always claimed a certain amount of clairvoyance.) The "difference" I was seeing was the serenity seen on the face of someone who has lived a long life and is now ready to move on, or that terminally ill patients have when they have truly accepted their approaching death and are completely comfortable with it. It was only then that I realized it was not Dodi's father who had put this play in motion; it was Diana herself. Diana had a standing invitation to join al Fayed on a cruise. Her time was up; Charles was going public with Camilla. What better time to yank the royal beard? She could give the Establishment a fright and have a wonderful time doing it. What better way to go?

Diana was ready. Her will was duly witnessed and filed. Her fairy princess dresses had been auctioned for her favorite charities. She had reconciled with her family members, even her stepmother. She and Charles had developed an amicable relationship—she had even become philosophical about Camilla. Most telling, that last year she had the glow, the serenity that most people have only at the end of a long satisfying life—or with the acceptance of the reality of terminal illness. There is no role for an ex-future Queen.

Will the monarchy continue on into the twenty-first century? King Farouk, the last King of Egypt, once said that by the turn of the century there would be only five kings left: the King of Hearts, the King of Diamonds, the King of Clubs, the King of Spades, and the King of England.

Everyone loves a parade—or a good show—and nobody does it better or on a larger scale than the British royals. Year after year, decade after decade, century after century—the British love it, but can they afford it? Are they willing to continue to pay the price? Do they even want to? When the Queen's parents married in 1923 and her father, the Duke of York, asked for his increased salary (due to his marriage) the country was economically depressed and unemployment was high. There was considerable complaining, but nobody ever really considered denying it.

British royalty dates back into the mists of antiquity, when Kings really ruled and princesses really lived in turreted castles—cold and drafty castles, but castles nevertheless. However, it was not until the reign of the fiery haired Tudor princess, Elizabeth I, that England became a power to be reckoned with. While publicly rebuking her wayward privateers, she was privately rewarding them with lavish praise and monetary rewards—maybe more. As a result England's coffers filled with gold and other treasures and she began to claim territories around the world. The British Empire had begun. It continued to grow and flourish, eventually adding Empress of India to Queen Victoria's list of titles. ("Lovely, lovely India," Queen Mary called it.) At the turn of the century it could still be said that "the sun never sets on British soil." Under such conditions, the British Empire not only could afford the cost of maintaining their royal family, they actually benefited from it. Besides, all nations had royalty. Even America had its Astors and Vanderbilts.

By the mid-18th century democracy was coming of age and the American colonies broke away from their English masters, although it took a costly, bloody war to do it. For the first time in recent history a representative government of the people, for the people, and by the people was established. It was an idea whose time had come.[5] No more kings, but a careful balance of executive, legislative, and judicial branches. France became a republic about the same time, followed by other nations around the world. Today there are fewer than thirty monarchs in the entire world (including tiny nations) and many of those have little or no power. So, from two perspectives—British history and world trends—monarchies are losing ground. The Russians brutally murdered theirs in 1917. Hitler took over in Germany in the '30's. India proclaimed her independence in 1947.

In addition, England has been economically depressed since World War I with continuing high unemployment, many doing without what most of us consider basic necessities. There is no longer a plethora of wealth flowing into the tiny nation from far flung colonies because there are no longer far flung colonies. On the basis of these facts alone the royals appear to be on their way out. Queen Elizabeth II could very well be the last British monarch. But this is not the whole story. People have a strong *need* for royalty—for the magic of royalty, the fairy-tale quality. Not just the British people; it seems to be a universal trait. (However, it is the British who have their King Arthur legends, their Henry VIII, Elizabeth I, Queen Victoria.) Americans would definitely love the British monarchy to continue on into the foreseeable future, but Americans are not paying the bill, we are only watching the show—and it is quite a bill. (It is impossible to determine the real cost because royalty with all its ceremonials brings in a lot of tourism money.)

Also, the British are very traditional. Royalty is a big part of their history, of who they are. Most of them don't really want to give that up, especially the generation that lived during World War II and bonded so strongly with their brave ruler, King George VI and his equally brave and very charming consort, Queen Elizabeth (the Queen Mother). In those days the King and Queen symbolized Britain, all that it was, all that it might be. The country was literally almost destroyed by German bombs, especially London. Four million buildings were destroyed by German bombs. The people didn't have enough food to fill their bellies or enough coal to warm their bodies, but the sight of the King and Queen—*their* King and Queen—inspecting the bomb damage, encouraging the homeless, risking their own lives to stay with their people, kept them going. There is something magic about royalty—at least there used to be. But that generation is gone or going. The younger generation, those who came of age with the Beatles, and all sorts of human rights movements, is a generation that is not so traditional, not so patriotic, not so willing to do without so that the royals can live like kings, which is what they do. Actually, many people were beginning to voice their opinions that royalty had outlived its usefulness *before* World War II. Even David, then Prince of Wales, later King Edward VIII and Duke of Windsor, felt that much of the ritual, the ceremony, was ridiculous and he said as much. He frequently commented that he would "modernize" the monarchy when he became king. Sounds very much like Diana—and may help explain why he did not remain King very long. The Queen, with Philip's help, has done more to modernize the monarchy than most people realize. She stopped the ritualistic presentation of debutantes at Court, among other things. However, at the time of Diana's death, even the Queen's mother and sister curtsied to her in public, and servants were required to back out of the royal presence. The courtiers do not like change; they do whatever they must to maintain the status quo. Former King Edward VIII told the Countess of Romanones that (then) Prime Minister Stanley Baldwin only used his relationship with the Duchess as an excuse to have him removed from the throne.[6] Having traveled widely, he was much more "modern" than the rest of this family and felt the monarchy could do without many ancient rituals and still be "royal."

But then the Big War came and the perfect royal family—the King, the Queen, and their two lovely daughters ("We four," the King always said) became a symbol and a beacon of hope to this tiny beleaguered nation. The Queen continued to use her incredible PR skills and at this time the Palace was still able to control the media. The public knew exactly what the Queen wanted them to know. They "knew," for example, that the royal family lived on the same slim war rations as the rest of the nation.[7] (The royal family had their own venison, trout, salmon, quail, strawberries, clotted cream, butter, etc. from Windsor and Balmoral.) And when the war was over, the ailing nation was delighted that their lovely Princess was to marry the handsome Philip (who was quickly de-Germanized) and were happy to provide additional clothing rations for her trousseau and to pay for the fabulous wedding and the honeymoon aboard the royal yacht, *Britannia*. The wedding cost millions but it provided a happy diversion from the nation's trials and tribulations and the money was considered well spent, at least by most people. (It also brought in millions in tourism and preparation.) During this period the royal family represented solid middle class family values and were revered for it. Their role has changed. England never fully recovered economically from World War II. (She really had not recovered from World War I when the new war began.) Maintaining the royal family in the style to which they are accustomed is extremely expensive. Already the Queen has become the first monarch in British history to pay income tax, although both Prince Charles and King George VI have at times returned part of their Civil List income to the Government. When Windsor Castle was badly damaged by fire[8] there was so much balking by taxpayers over the cost of restoration ("While it stood, it was theirs. When it burns it is ours.") that the Queen arranged for public tours of Buckingham Palace to help pay for the restoration. She also announced a cash bonus for those who helped save many priceless items. However, the Queen has a hard time turning money loose. Her income tax is on her public income only, not her vast private income. She decided to provide tours of the library in lieu of the cash bonuses, and when she agreed to cut the cost of running the royal residences she did it by cutting out perks for her staff. She cut out nothing for herself. She agreed to fly commercial instead of using the Queen's Flight, saving the taxpayers $3,000,000.00, but she only did it once. Still, since the death of the Princess she has made a greater effort. The Civil List will be cut tremendously until only the monarch, his or her spouse, their children, and their grandchildren in direct line of succession will be included. (Presently there are numerous aunts, uncles, and cousins receiving an annual salary from the Government.) By her death the Princess has made a real impact on the monarchy. Already the Queen has done things she never did before, simple things like visiting a pub, riding in a public taxi, more walk-abouts, in addition to the more significant moves. Since Diana's death curtsying is optional, Parliament has revised the Primogeniture law (with no opposition from the Queen), certain other changes to ceremony and procedure have been instigated. The Queen is making an effort to be more accessible, but as royal writer Brian Hoey concedes: "People no longer believe royalty walks on water." Pretty big change.

Will Charles be King? Yes, when his mother, Queen Elizabeth II, dies he will be King. For him not to be would require an act of Parliament, agreed to by the Queen,[9] that upon her death or abdication, the monarchy would end and a new head of state would be elected. It is extremely unlikely that this will happen. The Queen takes her role very seriously; it is not something to be casual about. Her father was also her King, and she perceives herself as having received a mandate, not only from her father, but from the people, to reign. It will take a lot to move her from this position—but then, a lot has happened. This is not the first time the Monarchy has been in question; it probably will not be the last time. Presumably, the act could alternatively provide for William to succeed rather than Charles. A better question might be, will Charles ever be crowned? Probably so. It depends on what happens between now and then. He has a better chance than he would have if Diana had lived and continued to push for the crown to go directly to William. Right now he is being perceived as having made a real effort to be the father his boys need now. Camilla was being kept out of sight at first. This is changing. He is gradually letting the people get used to seeing them together. He has a talent for "shooting himself in the foot." He never stopped seeing Camilla. Whether the people will accept her remains to be seen. While they might be willing to see her as his wife, it is less likely they will allow her to be Queen. In 1936, Sir Alan Lascelles said to King Edward VIII: "You can have the Throne or you can have the woman. You cannot have both." Times have changed, but perhaps not that much. Also, if it can be demonstrated that Diana did not die in an "accident," but was actually assassinated, that will have to be factored in, and will depend largely on where the actual blame lies—or rather where it is perceived to lie. It will certainly affect people's perception of the royal family, and of Charles in particular. It seems certain at this point that William will one day be King, and at a much earlier age than his father. He will possibly be one of the most popular monarchs ever. He seems to have all the best qualities of both his parents, in addition to the training and care of both the Queen and Prince Philip, greatly increased since their mother's death.

How are the boys handling this tragedy? Seemingly as well as could be expected at this point. It has not really been long enough to know. The first year they would have still have been in the shock and denial stages; only later comes the anger and depression, possibly guilt. William appears to be handling it better. This may be very misleading. He and his mother were very close. As he gets into the anger stage of the grief process he may become very rebellious and engage in self-destructive behaviors. More likely he is repressing his feelings to some degree. This is the royal way, but Harry's open grief may be healthier in the long run. The word is (from Richard Kay, royal journalist) that a Buckingham courtier has noted that "[since Diana's death] the royal family has taken Diana into their bosom." Now isn't that just ducky? Dead she is a wonderful wife, mother, future Queen of England; alive she was a loose cannon about to sink the royal ship. It is worth noting that, in spite of her brother's brave words at her funeral, the boys are gradually being weaned away from their mother's family. Diana's father is dead, her mother is ineffective, her brother is far away in South Africa. That only leaves her two sisters and, while they had considerable contact in the beginning, they are being distanced. The boys will be Windsors—but Spencer blood flows in their veins.

The boys already have many advantages over previous royal heirs. They have had a far more normal upbringing than any previous heirs.

The Queen was almost encapsulated during her formative years. Charles has had a somewhat more normal life. Still, he has always been surrounded by royal servants. Both boys were born in hospital (not the first royal babies to be, but the first ones so close to the throne). They had real hands-on parenting, not only as infants, but continuing on. Diana, especially, tried very hard to be sure they actually experienced "real life;" that they stood in line to get ice cream; that they played in the parks and playgrounds; and not just in traditional royal pursuits; that they saw real suffering, poverty, pain, so that as adults they will be able to relate to the people. Certainly the shock of their mother's untimely death will leave traumas, but hopefully they will have the resources to deal with it, and perhaps be stronger because of it. Looking ahead into the twenty-first century, it seems almost certain the handsome, charming, responsible William will one day sit on the throne of England. What *will* change will be the perks—and the power. They will continue to be the richest family in the nation; they will still be at the top of the heap socially, but the people will be less and less willing to pay for a way of life that no longer is acceptable in the world that Diana knew and wanted her boys to know—the real world.

7

DEATH OF A PRINCESS

They are healthy, happy boys, Princes of the Realm. At thirteen the elder is King of England, Edward V. It is better—for England—to eliminate possible dissension. He is much too young to rule. There can be only one King of England. Edward V and his brother, the Duke of York are taken to the Tower. A pillow over their face while they sleep will suffice. They feel no pain, no suffering. It is for the good of England. It must be done. I, Richard, am now King of England, Richard III.

When the Waleses's marital problems first began to be made public my granddaughter, rather embarrassed, asked, "They don't still cut off their heads, do they?" (She was old enough to know better.) I laughed and assured her they neither cut off their heads nor lock them in the Tower. I'm not laughing now.

During the first few days following the Princess's death, like millions around the world, I was in shock. I simply could not believe she was really dead. Gradually, especially after viewing the funeral for hours on end, I had to accept that she was dead. Gone.

"The Queen and the Prince of Wales are deeply distressed and shocked by the news."

— Buckingham Palace

"I am utterly devastated. The whole of our country, all of us, will be in shock and mourning. Diana was a wonderful, warm and

compassionate person who people, not just in Britain but throughout the world, loved and will be mourned as a friend. Our thoughts and prayers are with her family, particularly her two sons, and with all the families bereaved in this quite appalling tragedy."
—— British Prime Minister Tony Blair

"Beyond words…England has lost its real Queen."
—— Liz Smith, columnist

"The Duchess has lost someone she has always considered a sister and a best friend. There are no words strong enough to describe the pain in her heart."
—— statement from spokesman for Sarah Ferguson, Duchess of York

"A light that shined brightly has gone out…We will miss her"
—— Hillary Rodham Clinton, First Lady

"…She was a young woman of our times, warm, full of life and generosity. Her tragic death will be deeply felt…"
—— French President Jacques Chirac

"…a beacon of light has been extinguished."
—— Former Prime Minister Margaret Thatcher

As we absorbed the shock of the news of Princess Diana's death, except for the single terse statement from Buckingham Palace (the royal family were entrenched at Balmoral), there was a roaring silence from the royal family. We waited…Prime Minister Tony Blair issued a comforting message…it was announced that there would be no state funeral…but, rather, "a unique funeral for a unique person"…We waited…flowers began to pile up at Kensington Palace and other parts of London…long, long lines of people waited to sign the too few condolence books. By the third day newspaper headlines began to blast out: "Where Is Our Queen When We Need Her?" "Not One Word

Has Come From A Royal Lip, Not One Tear Has Been Shed In Public From A Royal Eye" (*The Sun*) and (from *The Daily Mirror*) "Your People Are Suffering. Speak To Us Ma'am." Charles, the forty-eight year old future King of England, had to argue with his mother, the Queen, to gain permission to go to France to escort the body of Diana, his children's mother, back to England. It was not appropriate, she argued.

More condolence books were provided, not only in London, but at British embassies around the world. It was announced that the service would be held in Westminster Abbey, the palace where kings are crowned—and laid to rest...the flowers piled higher...the procession would be lengthened from one mile to three and a half miles to allow more people to participate...Then, finally, there were pictures of Charles and the boys inspecting the flowers and greeting the people outside Balmoral Castle, expressing their gratitude for the prayers of the people. One heart-rending picture shows Harry clinging to his father's hand—or perhaps it was the other way around. (One of the earliest pictures was of Charles, accompanied by Diana's sisters, bringing her body back to England. He appeared totally devastated. Even in these circumstances, Sarah and Jane curtsied to the Prince of Wales.) Incredibly, the Queen planned to go ahead with a hunt scheduled that week. It was Charles who demanded it be canceled. It was the people who pushed her into action. It was William who finally asked, "Why are we here when Mummy's in London?" Why, indeed? This is an amazing demonstration of the Queen's "apartness" from her people. In August you go to Balmoral. Period. Funerals—state or otherwise—are not on the schedule. Throughout history, it has been when monarchs lose touch with the people that they lose their heads—or at least their thrones. One of the Queen's first actions was to call the Paris hospital not to inquire about her treatment or whether she suffered, but to inquire whether Diana was wearing any royal jewels and, if so, to return them immediately.[1] If this were a soap opera, the announcer would be saying "Will the Queen wake up in time to save her throne?" (The Queen did seem to get the message, but not until Charles gave her an ultimatum. The monarchy must be relevant and it must represent and reflect the people. Fifty years ago she told her advisors, "I must be seen to be believed." Today she must be seen to be *relevant*.)

Then it was announced that the Queen would be returning to London a day early—and that she would be speaking to the people. She was and she did. She let it be known that she was "hurt" that the people thought she was uncaring. This in itself was extremely unusual. Normally, the Queen does not publicly react to criticism. For the second time in her reign of forty-six years—except for the annual Christmas message begun by her grandfather in 1932, the Queen delivered a live television message to her subjects, saying, "I speak to you as your Queen and as a grandmother...I admire and respect her for her energy and commitment to others, and especially for her devotion to her two boys...In good times and bad, she never lost her capacity to smile and laugh, nor to inspire others with her warmth and kindness...a remarkable person, an exceptional and gifted human being." It seemed to satisfy the people (I was satisfied), but there was nothing in it of loving her, of losing her, of any sense of deeper grief. She was speaking of the woman whose name she had ordered not to be spoken in her presence—but she had sent flowers on her birthday. Charles and the boys greeted the mourners outside Kensington Palace and thanked them for their flowers and prayers. Later they made a private visit to the Chapel Royal in St. James Palace where Diana's coffin lay until it was moved to Kensington Palace on the eve of her funeral. Reportedly, she was laid to rest in a new black Katherine Walker coatdress. A rosary given her by Mother Teresa was beside her[2] and she was wearing several rings. According to one report, her face was unscarred and she "looked wrenchingly lovely." There were no public photos and no public viewing. The next day, as the funeral procession passed the royal family at Buckingham Palace, the Queen bowed her head,[3] the first time she had bowed to anyone since the death of her father, King George VI, in 1952. It was a historical moment, a pivotal moment for the monarchy. The Queen had at last acknowledged Her Royal Highness, Diana,

Princess of Wales, Queen of People's Hearts. Whether she did it out of genuine respect and grief, or whether it was the gesture of an astute politician, probably will never be known. Perhaps it was some of both. Although the Queen could be very irritated with Diana at times, they shared their love for the boys and concern for Charles's readiness for the throne. Certainly she was beginning to hear the message of the people. She, who never paid attention to opinion polls, was paying attention now. Although stripped in life of her royal trappings, Diana was still obviously "the people's Princess" and the Queen of People's Hearts—and the Queen made note of it. "The Palace" offered to restore her royal status posthumously, but her brother, now head of the family, in his terrible grief over the loss of this sister who had mothered him, refused it. He didn't say so, but clearly he was feeling it was too little too late.[4]

When the Queen left Buckingham Palace for Westminster Abbey her flag was lowered and *for the first time in history* the Union Jack was flown at half-mast. It was another sop to her grieving subjects. Another historical moment. The Queen's flag—not the Union Jack—flies over whatever residence she is in. When she leaves, it is lowered; when she enters another royal residence, it is raised, but this time when she left Buckingham Palace the Union Jack was raised to half-mast like all the other flags in the city—for the first time ever. Actually, her original plan had been to simply come down for the funeral and go back to Balmoral the same day, without ever entering Buckingham Palace; thus no flag would need to be flown.

The funeral itself was indeed a unique service for a unique person. No detail was overlooked and everything had a special significance. Considering the very short time available for preparation, and the total unexpectedness, the final production was amazing. By contrast, long before the Queen Mother died, her funeral plan had already been prepared in very elaborate detail. Diana's funeral was as elaborate and as carefully planned as her wedding had been, but instead of months, there were only days to plan. There was also no precedent. Never before had there been a funeral for a future Queen Mother and former future Queen. It was confusing. Since it was not a state funeral[5] there were no crowned heads (other than the Queen). Even President Clinton could not attend since he was a Head of State. The nearly two thousand invited guests included fashion leaders, artists, the Hollywood faction, but there were also representatives of the many charities she supported and very ordinary people she cared about. The invitation list was made from her Christmas card list with the help of her loyal butler, Paul Burrell, and her private secretary. Still, there was very little time to get the invitations printed and delivered. At first there were murmurs that Charles was not wearing black at the funeral—but then it turned out that he was wearing a suit which Diana had helped him pick out and which was a favorite of hers. His own personal silent tribute to the woman he raised to the level of international megastar—but then let her fall and break. Charles's grief was real. He appeared devastated—but it did not turn him from Camilla. (In fact, he told a friend that he "needed her more than ever.") For Diana's funeral, the Queen appropriately wore black as expected. However, few people were probably aware of the honor she bestowed by her choice of brooch. The Queen Victoria bow brooch was worn by both Queen Alexandra and Queen Mary on their coronation days. The Queen wore the same brooch for the funeral of her father, King George VI and her Uncle David, the former King Edward VIII. She has dozens and dozens from which to choose and could easily have selected a far less historic piece.

Behind her lead lined coffin[6] walked the five men in her life—her husband, her father-in-law,[7] her brother, and her two beloved sons. They did her proud. Behind the Princes and the Earl were 500 representatives of her various charities and organizations, who had been encouraged to wear tee shirts or sweat shirts with the logos of their respective organizations. Her coffin, covered with the royal standard, was borne on a ceremonial gun carriage, used only six times in this century—for three kings: Edward VII, George V and George VI, a former king (Edward VIII), Sir Winston Churchill, and Lord Louis, Earl

Mountbatten. This put her in very good company, and note that she was the only female.[8] The cortege passed under Wellington Arch which is reserved for monarchs. The Abbey bell tolled once each minute. On the flag draped coffin were three floral arrangements, said to be roses and lilies—or sometimes roses, lilies and tulips. I kept hoping that one of them was freesias, her favorite flowers and the ones used at her wedding breakfast. I like to think they were. The ones from William looked like freesias. Then there was the heartbreaking card with the one word, "Mummy." The three arrangements were from her boys and her family. Inside the Abbey Prince Philip and Prince Charles each laid a wreath at the foot of the catafalque. Prime Minister Tony Blair set the service on Saturday so that all who wished could participate. Huge television screens were set up in Hyde Park so that everyone could watch the actual service. Estimates of those watching the service world wide have been set as high as two and a half *billion*, up from the 750 million who watched the beautiful fairy-tale wedding sixteen years earlier.

The royal family appropriately did not take part directly in the proceedings. The boys had been allowed to decide if they wanted to walk in the procession. Charles and Prime Minister Tony Blair were in continuous communication and the boys were included in the planning. It seems to have been Charles who finally got the Queen to move. The service began on the dot of 11:00, with the British national anthem, "God Save the Queen"—a tribute that had been denied the Princess a few years before on her first post-separation visit to a foreign nation. Tony Blair read from St. Paul's letter to the Corinthians—the same passage of love that had been read in St.Paul's Cathedral sixteen years before at her wedding. George Carey, Archbishop of Canterbury, in his opening prayer, gave thanks…"for her sense of joy and for the way she gave so much to so many people…for her vulnerability, for her radiant and vibrant personality, for her ability to communicate warmth and compassion, for her ringing laugh and above all for her readiness to identify with those less fortunate in our nation and in our world…In her life Diana profoundly influenced this nation and the world." I wondered if ever before an Archbishop of Canterbury had spoken at a funeral using the person's familiar name. Each of her sisters spoke, but it was her brother Charles, Earl Spencer, who delivered the eulogy, placing the blame for Diana's death squarely on the shoulders of the media, but not excusing the royal family. Inside and outside the Abbey unprecedented sustained applause erupted. Spontaneous applause in Westminster Abbey! Elton John, a good friend of the Princess, sang a revised version of "Candle in the Wind,"[9] leaving no dry eyes inside or out—not even his own. (A rock star in Westminster Abbey!) There was also, appropriately for the Princess of Wales, the Welsh national anthem. Prince William selected "I Vow to Thee, My Country," his mother's favorite hymn, and the lovely Verdi's Requiem, another favorite of Diana's. Charles also chose a hymn and probably organized all the music as he did for their wedding. It was William who suggested having Elton John sing. Robert Fellowes deserves a lot of credit. Being both the Queen's Private Secretary and Diana's brother-in-law, he was in a position to balance the wishes of both families with protocol. Over the years he had caused the Princess much anguish. Now he had a chance to make it up to her and the results seemed to please everyone. Prime Minister Tony Blair also worked continuously with Charles and the others involved to make it a special tribute. It truly was a unique funeral for a unique person.[10] The service that was surely was not the service that was first planned—rather it evolved in response to the demands of the people. For once, the Queen bowed to the demands of the people, not the other way around. Following the service, the Princess was taken to her family estate of Althorp, where, in a very private ceremony, she was supposedly laid to rest, not beside her father in the family mausoleum at St. Mary the Virgin Church, but on a man-made island with the family dogs. It was said that villagers feared being overrun by tourists if she was buried in the church; that it would become a "Graceland situation."

Even Diana's strongest supporters were unprepared for the unprecedented outpouring of love and grief around the world; by the intensity and magnitude of the grief, even as we were the ones who grieved. It was never clearer that the genius of Princess Diana was her ability to make people feel a connection to her, even those who never met her or ever expected to. The very Reverend Dr. Wesley Carr, Dean of Westminster Abbey put it this way, "Although a princess, she was someone for whom, from afar, we dared to feel affection, and by whom we were all intrigued." The Queen also began to understand that, in an age of popular media, the monarch must be seen to have a closer relationship with the people; to be capable of showing feelings. It has often been said that "in the mystique is the magic," "the light must never be let in on the monarchy;" yet, Diana, the most open, the most approachable, of all the royals, was also the one who most provided the magic. And it was the death of Diana that shattered the crystal moat protecting the royal mystique.

8
UNANSWERED QUESTIONS

"Oh, my lord, my lord!"

"Oh, my sweet Queen!" He is here now, my love...I take his face in my hands and kiss him, but it is a Judas kiss. He has raised an army against me. I warned him, I told him to his face—anything against myself I can pardon, but never an assault upon my throne. Robert Devereaux, my sweet Robert, Lord of Essex, has betrayed me. He has had a fair trial with honorable judges. The verdict is inescapable. I, I Elizabeth, I must sign this warrant for his death. It is for England, for the good of England. It must be done.

As time went on there were questions—unanswered questions—a lot of them. There is a time to be born and a time to die. When someone dies well before their natural time it is much harder to come to terms with. And when that person is a charismatic princess of the people there is a compelling need to deny it. When it can no longer be denied, there is anger, even rage. When the death results from an ordinary drunk-driving accident, there is a sense that it should never have happened, that it didn't have to be and we begin looking for reasons, for causes. It is too frightening to be reminded that, in spite of fame and riches and power, life can be arbitrarily snuffed out in a moment.

Still, in regard to Diana's death, there are too many unanswered questions. Where were all the witnesses? Wasn't the tunnel supposed to have been full of photographers on motorcycles, tourists in cars? Where were they? Why weren't they talking? What about the white Fiat? Wouldn't it have to be demolished? What happened to it? Why couldn't they get Diana out sooner? Why were the traffic cameras in the tunnel turned off? For that matter, how could it possibly happen that someone who was drunk was driving the Princess—and at such high speeds? Why did it take the French Government more than two years to decide it was a simple case of reckless driving? *(Is the investigation over?)* Why wasn't the Princess in surgery within *minutes*—instead of hours? How is it that the only survivor can't remember anything?

How is it possible that an armored[1] Mercedes can be demolished in a tangle with a Fiat and the Fiat escape unscathed? At least, it was able to get out the way—and fast. Too, too many questions! The Princess was well trained in surviving even terrorist attacks. She would never have failed to fasten her seat belt. It seems inconceivable that she would be without a seat belt. She was obsessive about seatbelts. (If the car was outrunning the photographers—at high speeds—how were the photographers able to see that her seat belt was not fastened?) Presumably her companion, the bodyguard, and the chauffeur were equally trained in surviving terrorist attacks. The life mission of the two men in the front seat of the car was to protect the Princess and her companion. Besides, if Henri Paul had been that intoxicated it would have been obvious and he would never have been allowed to drive. For that matter, with his training, he would not have allowed himself to drive. He not only "allowed" himself; he went back to the hotel for that very purpose. But assassination? Murder of the glamorous young mother? Impossible!

Think again. When Diana's bodyguard, Barry Mannakee, with whom Charles believed she had become too familiar, was killed in a motorcycle accident just eight months after he had been transferred from her service, she immediately thought that he had been killed by the M I5—*at the instigation of the Prince*. It does not matter if he was or not. What is important is that she believed this to be a possibility. (It is generally agreed that she eventually accepted that his death was an accident. What she actually said was, "I've always had a question about his death and I've been given an answer..." She does not say what that answer was.) She knew that Charles was furious that she had talked to him about their marital problems. (Charles failed to see that his discussing the problems with Camilla was no different—but, then, he failed to see a lot of things.) It seemed too much of a coincidence that he died so conveniently. Was he planning to write a book, maybe? (Incidentally, Charles's other confidante, Dale "Kanga," Lady Tryon, also died unexpectedly—quietly—in hospital. Was *she* going to write a book?)[2] But why would anyone want Princess Diana killed? With her beauty, her glamour, her good works, who could possibly want her done away with? The British Establishment, that's who.

She had become a threat to the monarchy—not to the Queen personally, but to the institution. She was steadily becoming more popular (read powerful) than the Prince—and not just in England, but around the world. But, you say, things like that just don't happen, not in modern times, not outside the movies and thriller mysteries. But they do. All the time those who get in the way of power, those who rock the boat, are wiped out. We accept this in the Mafia (Diana sometimes referred to the Palace as "the Mafia"—"The difference in the Mafia and the royals is these muggers wear crowns.") or in the drug culture, but not in the royal family! They are such *nice* people! They are nice people, and individually, would never do such a thing, but they are not in control. "The Establishment" includes all the courtiers, advisors, aides, assistants involved in operating the vast royal firm. When Prince Charles once said, "We don't run our staff, they run us," he spoke more truly than probably he knew. History has clearly shown that the royals will do *whatever* is necessary to maintain the status quo. (Remember how the courtiers banded together to prevent Prince Philip from having "undue" influence over the young Queen? They didn't want him giving her ideas—*they* would decide what she should and shouldn't do.) Monarchs believe they have a mandate to reign, originally a divine right, now a mandate from the people. When the royal match was made, with her shy charm and innocent past, Diana seemed to be perfect for producing an heir (and more) and would in no way interfere with Charles's way of life. The Monarchy has not survived a thousand years by being nice.

Diana was never supposed to have been an important person in her own right. On the joint television interview early in their marriage she said, "I feel my role is supporting my husband whenever I can, and always being behind him, encouraging him..." (Even the Queen Mother, influential as she was, worked through her husband, or his advisors, allowing herself to be seen by the public only as a wife and mother.) Diana was carefully chosen for the role via a royal selection process as cold and prosaic as any thoroughbred auction. At age nineteen she had the lineage, the upbringing and the docility to appear to meet the requirements for a future Queen of England. She was the first English bride of the heir to the throne in 700 years. She was even approved by his mistress, who saw no threat to her own relationship to the Prince in this shy, awkward girl. Camilla called her a "mouse," but she didn't stay a mouse. Overnight, it seemed, the Princess became a megastar. Nobody was prepared for this—not the Press, not the Royals, certainly not Diana herself. Everybody wanted to see *her*, read about *her*, hear what *she* was wearing, moaning if they ended up on Charles's side of the road. Charles tried to make light of it, especially in public, making remarks such as, "I'm just the collector of flowers these days," or apologizing for having only one wife—not enough to go around. But privately he was furious. After all his years of training and preparation here was this *girl* taking over the spotlight! As early as the first Australian tour in 1983 Press Officer Vic Chapman commented to a colleague: "We've got a problem. She's too popular, and he doesn't like it a bit." (Chapman later retired to Canada and has now died.)

Who are the MI6? They are the British Intelligence Service. (MI5 for internal affairs; MI6 for international affairs.) They are similar to our own CIA. They have tremendous power and autonomy because the very nature of their job requires complete secrecy. James Whitaker, noted royal writer, notes that they are "to all intents and purposes, out of control." Their job is to "defend the realm" and they do whatever they think is necessary to fulfill this duty. (Aline, Countess of Romanones, nee Griffith, notes concerning her own orientation as a spy for the United States during World War II, "We're accountable to only one guy—General Wild Bill Donovan. No government department has jurisdiction over our operations." This was over fifty years ago in the United States. She also explained that often, although working with a partner, neither really knew what the other was doing.) In other words, espionage is a totally covert activity, and as such, is subject to abuse. Modern sophisticated technology allows MI6 (and MI5) agents to know whatever they feel they need to know. Not only phone conversations have been recorded, but also private conversations within the royals' own homes. (It is now possible to take a picture of farmland from a space satellite that shows exactly what and how much lime, nitrogen, etc. needs to be added to the land and exactly where. Given that kind of technology, don't think they can't monitor our conversations any time they wish.) When the future King Edward VIII was seeing Wallis Simpson (in the 1930's), they began monitoring her phone calls "for national security"—she was thought to be sympathetic to the Nazis. Sophisticated surveillance of key people has continued ever since. They believe in protecting the royals from themselves, if necessary. Supposedly this is for their safety (and the country's safety), but such information can be misused. During wartime their role is clear—and necessary. In times of peace they may be inclined to become overzealous, and turn their excellent skills on the "enemy within." Still, why would Diana be a target—especially after she is divorced and demoted?

She was divorced and she was demoted, but as her brother, Charles, noted in his famous eulogy, she was not down. "Someone who was classless and who proved in the last year that she needed no royal title to continue to generate her particular brand of magic." Her star was clearly on the rise; Charles's was not. Yet it was as a result of Diana's death that he most clearly demonstrated his potential for Kingship. For once, he did not dither. It was he, *not the Queen*, who understood the temper of the people. It was he who demanded the Queen adjust her schedule for the week. It was he who finally gave the Queen an ultimatum: either she would make the necessary moves to properly mourn the Princess of Wales or he would go on television and apologize for the lack of response from the Queen. It was probably the first time in his life that he really stood up to his mother, the Queen, for what he truly believed to be right. He did the right thing.

Was the Queen really so uncaring? The Queen's life is ruled by protocol and has been since she was an infant. The Queen Mother's immediate response to the news of Diana's death was to remind the Queen that Diana was "not royal." Perhaps the Queen was only reacting to her training. More likely she was in shock like all the rest of us. She was trained from early childhood not to show emotion in public. When her beloved father, King George VI, died, only Philip—and her faithful servant, Bobo—saw her grief. Still, there is little evidence of any real grief, or even normal dismay over the death of a young mother. She did, appropriately wear black on that first Sunday at Crathie Kirk, as did the Queen Mother—but that is protocol. She did not rescind the order not to mention Diana's name in her presence. She had sometimes referred to her as "that silly girl." She probably honestly saw no reason why Diana should have the kind of funeral kings (and Winston Churchill) had. This did not mean that she did not feel her death was tragic; just that she did not see Diana as "majestic," or perhaps as having earned a royal funeral.

Diana has talked repeatedly about "modernizing the monarchy" (so have Prince Philip, the Duke of Windsor, and various others, but unlike her predecessors, Diana had the attention of the world); she has been accused of saying Prince Charles is not fit to be king (what she actually said is that she is not sure he *wants* to be king—but she also said "that 'the top job' would bring enormous limitations to him...she was not sure he could adapt"); she would like to see the crown pass directly to William. When the crown passes, presumably the Queen will be dead. Diana would have a great deal of influence on the young King William. Some would consider such an outspoken desire to be treason; apparently someone did. Add to this that they believe Diana is about to marry, not just a foreigner, but the son of a detested Egyptian Muslim, who has tried unsuccessfully to buy his way into British aristocracy. His son, Dodi, would be stepfather to the future King of England. Any children of *this* marriage would be stepsiblings to the Princes. How do they know Diana's marriage plans? They are monitoring her phone calls—and she is calling her close friends on that final day of her life. (Actually, they know that she is *not* about to marry Dodi, but if the public thinks she is, so much the better for them.) Add to this incendiary intrigue a fanatic person or persons. All it takes is for the Prince or the Queen to make an innocent remark such as "We can't let this happen" or "She has got to be stopped," and these fanatic defenders of the realm take it quite literally. They make sure she is stopped. They have tried everything else. Only one thing is left.

It is interesting to re-read the Diana stories with hindsight.

Sarah, Duchess of York, writes: "{The System} thought the Palace machine would grind me down; that I would surrender and then I would leave...I did leave..."(Diana did not.) Of the Men in Grey, she says, "The Firm's job was to perpetuate their own power. More royal than the Royals, the courtiers run the snootiest club in Britain. Their hostility toward outsiders was legend. In Victoria's day, they referred to Prince Albert as 'that German.'"

Lady Colin Campbell put it more bluntly: "[The courtiers] knew what was best for the country, and woe betide anyone who forgot that"—and she was writing about the days of King Edward VIII. She also wrote: "The Princess [Diana] is not more powerful than the Monarchy." (At the same time, James Whitaker was saying she is in "a no-lose situation," but of course, she couldn't win either—except by dying.)

Even Prince Philip, the Queen's husband, was not immune. In the early days of his marriage, as he tried to modernize the archaic methods and traditions of Buckingham Palace, he was blocked wherever he turned. The courtiers resisted any change—then and now. The courtiers (and the Queen Mother) did all they could to minimize Philip's influence on the young Queen. He was "too modern."

Royal writer James Whitaker writes: "Those in government departments who are keen to preserve the status quo see an independent Princess of Wales, freed from day-to-day strictures of court life, as a *growing threat*....they *fear she has the power* to undermine the House of Windsor...*a royal rogue who threatens the very existence* of the constitution of this country." (Italics are mine.) Remember, all this was written *before* she died—and it is pretty strong.

From Penny Thornton, Astrologer to the Princess: "If [Charles] was to have any chance at all of gaining the love and respect of the people, he had to walk out from under Diana's shadow. And that meant she had to go; she had to disappear from the headlines."

And to Diana, Thornton says: "...there are certain people in positions of power who believe you are a loose cannon on the deck of the royal family, and if you could be pushed over the brink, it would solve a lot of problems."

Both the Camillagate tapes and the Squidgy tapes were obviously "planted" for somebody to pick up and sell to the media, so who are they after? Is somebody using Charles *and* Diana to get to the *monarchy*? Sarah, Duchess of York, makes an interesting comment, not elaborated on: "As yet unwritten is the tale of how some of the most trusted people at Buckingham Palace have undermined the monarchy itself." She also notes that she was "the maiden for the pyre" but, in fact, she was only the opening act; it was Diana who was the lamb for the slaughter.

Then there was the strange story about Diana "hounding" art dealer, Oliver Hoare, with numerous, often anonymous phone calls, all coming from her office, or Charles's office, even though Diana was able to prove that many times she was somewhere else at least when some of the calls were made. What was this all about? Another attempt to make her look "unstable"? (It is possible, given the intensity of her needs coupled with the strength of her training that she could have made the calls and truly had no conscious memory of it. She would then continue to repeat the action because her needs had not been met—but she would not consciously remember that she had under normal conditions.)

Lady Colin Campbell: "While Diana was dealing with her separation, the courtiers were plotting her demise."

The Queen Mother to Diana's grandmother, "We have a *traitor* in our midst." (And she meant Diana—grandmother didn't want to lose her well-established standing in the royal family.)

Now Diana is about to marry the son of the detested Mohammed Al-Fayed (or so it appears), who will then become the stepfather of the future King of England. Can this woman be *allowed* to live?

The word to the press about Sarah was "The knives are out at the Palace for Fergie"—but Fergie left quietly. (Even the Queen, when asked what would happen should the Monarchy end, said, "We'll go quietly.") But Diana announced to the world, via her television interview, "I won't go quietly." The Prince noted very generously that he "didn't want to do anything [about Diana]. He was worried about her volatile and emotional state and it would be unfair to attack her." Pretty strong attack. His press person, Penny Junor, describes Diana as "paranoid" in her suspicions about Charles's relationship with Camilla Parker-Bowles (Diana was right on target), "jealous" when he spent time on royal duties and prone to "petulant tantrums." Quite a hatchet job there. All these people knew about Camilla all along: the Queen, Prince Philip, Charles's valet, detective, staff, friends who provided "safe houses" for the couple. In addition to all her other feelings, Diana felt humiliated that "everyone" knew about Charles's paramour.

Although Diana denied it, Charles has said that Diana *threatened*: (italics are mine) "You will never be King. I shall destroy you." In the heat of a divorce settlement people say many things.

When Diana was willing to give up her title, her friends urged her to keep it. Without it she would be obliged to curtsy to those who had only recently curtsied to her—including her sons. She would need her title for clout, they argued. They said "the title of HRH gave her protection *against being run over*." Interesting choice of words.

Her legal representative reported (after completing negotiations): "At the end of the day, it became clear that the *lamb was going to be fleeced*.""(Before being sacrificed?)

Diana herself spoke of "whispering campaigns." "enemies," "a grand scheme" to force her out of public life. "They" were out to get her; her phones were tapped. But, then, she was *paranoid*—or was she? She kept a paper shredder handy and used a scrambler on her phone. For really sensitive calls, she used a pay phone. She had her apartment swept for "bugs." (They don't need bugs these days; they have far more sophisticated equipment, but Diana didn't know this.) She was terrified that she would be declared mentally ill and "put away," her children taken from her. This was no idle fear. Both her mother and Fergie's mother had lost their children, as Diana well knew. ("And they were saying that I was unstable and needed to be put away in order to get better.")

Fergie to Diana: "They are out to get us—especially Bellowes {Robert Fellowes, the Queen's Private Secretary, Diana's brother-in-law, and Fergie's cousin}. First me, then you." Diana, too, distrusted her brother-in-law and all the courtiers, believing they were trying to destabilize her. Anne, the Princess Royal, and her husband, Timothy Laurence, moved out of Buckingham Palace to get away from the influence of the Grey Men—and Princess Anne was *born* royal.

Many comments *after* her death are of interest. We have already noted that, reportedly, one of the Queen's first questions was, not what kind of treatment she had or whether she suffered greatly, but whether or not Diana was wearing royals jewels when she died.

Al Fayed: "The strength and cruelty of the Establishment voices denying that theirs was true love strengthens my conviction that there were people in England determined that the woman who had been ejected from the royal family and stripped of her title of Royal Highness should not be allowed to marry my son." (There is considerable evidence that the Palace continued to monitor Diana's romances and "take care of" any that were undesirable. Pakistani heart surgeon, Hasnat Khan, was considered unsuitable; so was James Gilbey.)

Reportedly, the first person Charles called on learning of Diana's death was not the Queen, but—you guessed it—Camilla. Only after talking to her did he inform the Queen, who was under the same roof (Balmoral), of the horrific death of her ex-daughter-in-law, the mother of her grandsons.

Louise Berlioz, Lyon, France: "This is a funeral that has immobilized an entire people, even people of the world."

Donata Cilandi, 60 year old nurse, Venice, Italy: "It touches the bottom of my heart."

Russian President Boris Yeltsin, during the celebration of Moscow's 850th anniversary: "We remember that in Britain there is tragedy."

Mother Teresa: "Diana had a beautiful spirit." (Mother Teresa herself died before Diana was buried.)

Stockholm's tennis stadium: Mother with tennis racquet to son: "Shh! It's Diana's funeral."

Truly it was a loss felt round the world, and notice how people tended to speak of her as just "Diana," as if everyone knew who she was, or as if she might be family or a close friend; she needed no title or last name.

Many journalists (at this point the paparazzi were being blamed for the death) made a number of comments about Diana "using," "manipulating" the media for her own purposes. She did. As she herself stated, if they were always going to be there why not use them? Besides, they were her only means of defense. If Anne Boleyn had had this resource, her story might have been different.

To summarize our case:

1. We have established that the Royal family will do whatever is necessary to maintain their position, whether it entails breaking away from the Pope and setting yourself up as Head of the Church of England, signing an execution order, sending your cousin and his family to terrible execution, changing your family name, or exiling a member of the family.

2. The Prince was quite content as he was. He had everything he wanted or needed. He had no need to marry. He lived like a...well, like a Prince.

3. He was, however, a dutiful Prince and he had a duty to provide an heir to the throne of England. For this he had to marry a young Protestant virgin of either royal or aristocratic blood. (She would, after all, be the next Queen of England—a very prestigious position.)

4. He finds the perfect person—young, aristocratic, photogenic, empathic. She was in love with the Prince of Wales (not necessarily the same as Charles—she hardly knew Charles), about whom she had daydreamed during her somewhat unhappy adolescence. She leaned on his every word, catered to his every whim, consoled him when he discussed his burdens and frustrations.

5. He courted her in a very sporadic fashion, considering the pros and cons very carefully and maintaining his intimate relationship with Camilla—who was their constant chaperone.

6. Everybody, including his parents, is pressuring him make a decision. She seems perfect for the role in a shy and quiet kind of way.

7. With the approval of his confidante (who sees the pudgy, unworldly teenager as no threat), he proposes. She accepts. He continues his life with Camilla as he prepares to participate in the Wedding of the Century, actually spending his wedding eve night with her.

8. Diana becomes aware of his relationship with Camilla but, with youthful confidence, believes (hopes?) she can "win" him away from her. After all, she will be his wife; his Queen consort, the mother of his children.

9. She becomes pregnant on her rather prolonged honeymoon. (After all, that was why he married her.) She is not quite so shy and pliable and he needs a lot of advice from Camilla. Diana becomes more and more upset over his continuing relationship. He promised her before they married that he would give it up—or she thought he did.

10. She quickly became the star of the show—and Charles did not like playing sidekick. As early as the first Australian tour, her press officer noted that there was a problem—she was "too popular."

11. The marriage falls apart, apparently because Charles was unwilling to give up any part of the life he had before marriage and Diana was unable or unwilling to live a lie. There were also other tremendous pressures; in addition to all the pressure any young parents are subjected to, they had their heavy load of royal duties and the constant media intrusion.

12. At first Diana is too intimidated by the crowds, the protocol, the Queen, Charles, to do little more than chew her nails. (They are chewed—check the early pictures.) Gradually her survival instincts kick in and she begins to fight back.

13. She courts the media—she can't escape them, she might as well use them to her advantage. She finally acknowledges her illness and seeks help. This gives her some feeling of control over her life, but she is terrified that she will be declared mentally ill by "them" and will be "put away." She seems never to have considered the block, only the Tower. (However, Dodi's father has been quoted as saying that she told him that "one day she would go up in a helicopter and not come down.")

14. Because of her very real fear of being "committed" ("Friends on my husband's side were indicating that I was again unstable and should be put in a home of some sort in order to get better."), in desperation she allows a book to be written that puts the Prince in a very bad light—among other things it pictures a Prince who is a poor father, an adulterous husband, unsuited to be King. She has created a constitutional crisis—but gradually she is tapping into her inner strength. She is changing from victim to victor.

15. Ever mindful of the popularity of the Princess, the Queen insists the royal show must go on. There must be a show of unity.

16. Still the end is not yet. First there are the tapes, Squidgy and Camillagate, then the Prince's television interview (which is intended to improve his tarnished image) during which he admits to adultery—not a lot of help for his image.

17. There is first a legal separation, but by now there is too much anger; too much retaliation. There must be a divorce.

18. Every effort is made to make Charles look better and Diana look worse. She is stripped, not only of her title, but her ladies-in-waiting, her use of royal transportation. (Actually, she was still allowed to use the Queen's Flight and other royal facilities for some occasions.) Charles was angry. He wanted *everything* taken away from her. The Queen was not so punitive. Diana herself dismissed her

bodyguards. When various organizations asked for her they were told that she was not available, but the Prince was. When she asked to go to Saudi Arabia, they told her it was too dangerous. Instead they sent Charles and she was sent to Germany to comfort the wives and families. She was invited to present the prestigious Richard Dimbleby Lecture, giving her view of AIDS, but courtiers intervened and the invitation was withdrawn. She asked to go to Northern Ireland to comfort parents of a child killed by an IRA bomb. Prince Philip was sent instead. It is Diana, one lone woman, against one of the richest and most powerful families in the entire world—and the courtiers.

19. The plan was to gradually fade her out of the picture. They have the heirs; they don't need her any more. Reportedly, the Queen had all her memorabilia removed from the castle gift shops. Seems unnecessarily tacky (and unlike the Queen, but Charles might have insisted or it might not be true). Certainly her name was removed from the royal "prayer list"—surely she still needed the prayers of the people. The Sunday at Craithie Kirk (Church) near Balmoral just hours after her death, with her sons in the congregation, her name was *not mentioned* by the priest—not in comment and not in prayer.[3] While the whole world mourned the boys were required to attend church as if nothing had changed. So bizarre was it, that at one point young Harry asked his father, "Are you sure Mummy is dead?"

20. She continued to gain popularity while the Prince was losing ground. It is the Prince who is heir to the throne. There are political implications. One of her biggest fans is now Labour Prime Minister, Tony Blair—the Prime Minister who promised, that if elected, no £80,000 royal yacht would be built "while people are queuing up for hospital beds." He won by a landslide victory. Her boyfriend's father has been credited with helping pull down the previous Conservative (pro-royalist) government of Prime Minis-

ter John Major. It is Blair's government that allowed Diana to go into Bosnia. It was to be announced in September that she would be Britain's International Ambassador, a role she had long wanted and which the Palace had refused her. There may be more. Certainly manufacturers of land mines were affected.

21. Apparently, there has been no concerted effort by the British Government to find out what really happened. She is not only a British subject, but also the future Queen Mother, a former future Queen, and they are just accepting, with all these unanswered questions, that this was a simple case of drunk driver accident? Can the British government, in fact, conduct an objective investigation if their own Secret Intelligence people are responsible? Is the French Intelligence Agency involved, too? The CIA? The French government did conduct an intensive investigation, but more than two years after the "accident" the official report of the investigation provided more questions than answers. They have a dilemma. They cannot ignore the unanswered questions, yet how can they "rat" on a sister nation? Worse than that—she died in France, in a French hospital, in the care of French physicians, under very questionable procedures. She died *after* the accident. The very people who were supposed to save her life let her die. Had they been mere citizens, they could have been charged with manslaughter. They must protect themselves.

How was it done, the assassination? I don't know. I know that the royals will go to any lengths to preserve their position, their status quo—or the royalists will do it for them. (In no way do I mean to imply that the Queen or Prince Charles were instigators of this plan.)

I was not around when Henry VIII was executing people, nor when his daughter Mary killed off all her opponents, or…But I know about Nicolas II, Tsar of Russian and his family's brutal assassination. I know about Edward VIII and his lifetime exile. I know about Peter Townsend. I know that Diana was being perceived more and more as a threat to the monarchy, especially to Charles as she voiced her concern regarding his "fitness" for the role of King (his mother had similar reservations at times, one reason she has not been willing to abdicate in his favor, but that is different). Perhaps Paul Henri, her chauffeur on that fateful night, was drugged. A lot of alcohol got into his body in a relatively short time. Maybe the limousine was tampered with.[4] The speedometer was "stuck"—what causes a speedometer to stick? There were reports in the hours and days immediately following her death that "paparazzi" on motorcycles were interfering with the driving—dashing in front of the vehicle, darting in and out. (Supposedly, the Mercedes was outrunning the motorcycles—so how could they be in front of it, or beside it?) Maybe they only looked like paparazzi—and what about the white Fiat Uno that was involved with the accident and then just totally disappeared from sight? How can that be explained? It has to have been disposed of, otherwise it would have been found by now.[5] Diana was still alive after the accident. She was, in fact, killed by the French medical personnel. They must protect themselves. Unfortunately, she did not speak French (it was one of the things she was criticized for, after all French is the "language of Kings") so anyone trying to help might not have understood if she said anything. (Also, she was intubated soon after the crash, so speech was not possible.) Someone on the scene said she appeared "agitated." I would probably be agitated, too, if I was being murdered. It has been widely reported that her life could have been saved if the emergency had been handled differently, if they had gotten her to surgery much more quickly. Why didn't they? A lot of "explanations" have been provided concerning the different methods of handling emergencies in different countries. It seems obvious to me that with an injury of this nature, of this severity, with a future Queen Mother, she should have gotten to surgery much, much more quickly. Then she would at least have had a fighting chance. She might still be alive and smiling today. (With all the explanations of how in France, "the ER is sent to the victim," the ambulance is equipped with fully trained doctors and emergency needs, yet Christopher Andersen states that, "*As soon as he saw her,* Dr. Riou knew she was bleeding to death internally." (My italics.) Why did no one else recognize this? Her blood pressure was falling steadily. If this was a trauma team, shouldn't they have known that? There seems to be a lot of confusion about who called and which call(s) were responded to. I have two scenarios in my head. In one there is the lone crushed limousine with its four victims and a lone doctor comes to attend them; in the other scenario the tunnel is *teeming* with people—passing cars, motorcycles, dozens of paparazzi, lots of people. Why did *no one* see what happened? Why are there no pictures? Paparazzi were popping off hundreds of photos.

If this were anybody but royalty, a lot would have been made of the fact that Charles may very well have been spared a great deal of money. The divorce settlement of $26,000,000.00 was to have been paid out over a five year period, plus an additional $660,000.00 annually for her office and staff. She lived less than one year after the settlement. Probably he will still have to pay the money to her estate which her boys will inherit (but not the $660,000.00 yearly.) Who will control it? Former Prime Minister John Major has been appointed guardian. (Major is a royalist.)

There is another point. Horrendous as it is, it must be mentioned. Diana was shorn of Her Royal Highness status, but she was allowed to keep her title of Princess of Wales. Charles is divorced now, legally free to marry Camilla (who is also now divorced), but there cannot be two Princesses of Wales.[6] Put another way, Charles, as King will be Head of the Church of England. (Henry VIII had himself proclaimed Head of the Church in 1533 and every monarch since has been heir to that title.) As such he can not marry a second time in the church as long as he has a living wife. Since the Church does not recognize divorce, in the eyes of the Church, a wife is a wife as long as she lives. So in the eyes of the Church, Charles is now a widow and therefore can remarry. There is still the question of whether a divorcee can be crowned

Queen—or for that matter, whether an adulterous Prince can be crowned. And Camilla, so far, still has a living husband.

I don't know what happened that night in the tunnel in Paris. Perhaps we will never know for sure, but a lot is known. I stayed glued to the television all week. Scenes were shown and reshown. Information—and funeral plans—changed almost hourly. But some facts *are* known. One of the most tantalizing is that a white Fiat was involved in the accident, probably *caused* the accident, and then just totally disappeared, not a trace was ever found. There was also a motorbike involved in the accident which also has never been found.

Another fact, that would have immediately provided all the information, is that the video cameras used inside the tunnel to monitor traffic were off when the accident happened. I wonder how frequently this happens.

As Diana and Dodi were leaving the hotel, with Henri Paul driving, the guards saw a man using a cell phone about a block from where Diana's car exited. It was generally assumed that he was alerting the paparazzi—but it could have been a much more sinister message. Certainly their phone calls had been monitored closely by the MI6 (and Diana had made quite a few). They would know their plans, even with all the changes. They would now know exactly where they were headed and the route they would take—and when they would be in the tunnel. (The tunnel was not the shortest route to their destination. Why did they go that way?)

Photographer Romuald Rat was in pursuit (on a motorcycle with a driver). Although he claimed not to have seen the accident, but came up on it immediately, he did not call for help. (In addition to common decency, French law requires bystanders to call authorities if they witness an accident or someone in danger.) Rat did not call because, he said, he heard that someone else already had called. If he was the first one on the scene, who was supposed to have called—and who told him that someone else had called? Sounds like when Adam and Eve's children went forth and married—whom? And why didn't he call anyway, just to be sure? People were *dying*! Why! The French police did hold seven photographers and drivers for several days, but if they learned anything of importance it has not yet been made public. In fact, very little has been officially made public. There seems to be a lot of confusion as to who called and who responded. The first person on the scene, Eric Petel, was unable to get the police to take him seriously. One person was said to have heard the crash and "came downstairs" to see what happened. He was supposed to have called for help. How do you come downstairs and see into a concrete tunnel?

Another driver, Francois Le`vy, was in front of Diana's car. He told reporters that he saw in his rear view mirror what he thought was a motorcade, because the motorcycles were on either side of the Mercedes. Then one motorcycle began to "fishtail" in front of the car. The Princess and Dodi were in the back seat—why would a photographer try to get in *front* of their car? He saw what he *thought* was a very bright flashbulb. It could have been something much worse. (Several people mentioned this extremely bright light, the flash that Michael Tomlinson spoke of.) As the motorcycle zoomed ahead, the Mercedes veered to the left, to the right, to the left again and then crashed. (According to another report another car forced the Mercedes into the concrete pillar—the white Fiat?) At the sound of the explosive crash Lev`y stopped (at the tunnel exit) and "a motorcycle went past me fast with two men on it." Again, it was assumed that the men were photographers escaping with their exclusive pictures—but it could have been her assassins.

Henri Paul apparently showed no signs of drunkenness either to Diana and Dodi or on the security cameras prior to driving. (More recently there have been reports that he also had more carbon monoxide than can be accounted for since he is assumed to have died instantly.)

The only survivor, Trevor Rees Jones, could not communicate with authorities at first because his lips and tongue had been cut off by the "accident." (How ironic can you get?) Later he could not remember anything. The facts don't fit here at all. Could he have been paid off? Threatened? His family threatened? The one person in the world who might be able to provide the truth is not talking—and is not being made to talk.

Michael Tomlinson, former MI6 agent, claims the accident is very similar to one which was planned for the assassination of Slobodan Milosavic of Yogoslavia.

Almost two hours elapsed from the moment of impact until surgery—two hours in a situation in which minutes were critical. Not only was she not rushed to the hospital, the rescue team was actually making matters worse by—in an apparent attempt to revive her—actually putting pressure on the torn pulmonary vein, causing more bleeding. (Was this part of a conspiracy? And the delay in calling for help?)

There is more. There might have been more links with the Fayeds than we know. His former brother-in-law, Adnan Khashoggi was an arms dealer. Diana's work with land mines was costing him a lot of money. We know that al Fayed was "black listed" by the British Establishment, supposedly for trying to bribe his way into British citizenship, into the aristocracy, actually. But he is also blamed for helping bring down the Conservative (pro-monarchy) government. Tony Blair, a strong supporter of Diana, then became Prime Minister of the Labour government, which is much more anti-royal, anti-status-quo. He saw Diana as the perfect representative of the New Britain he wanted to promote. It was through her clandestine relationship with Blair that she was able to pursue her dream of being an international ambassador for Britain. It was to be announced in September. This does not seem like something the Establishment is going to tolerate. One more reason she had to go.

Let's take a closer look at Henri Paul, the driver of the limousine, the driver with the high alcohol level, the man who has been labeled Diana's killer. According to Michael Tomlinson, former MI6 agent, Paul was on the MI6 payroll. Also according to Tomlinson, a similar assassination had been planned previously (one involving a tunnel).

Details were very similar. Henri Paul had gone off duty. On his own he went back to the hotel to take the couple to the apartment. He had called the hotel repeatedly to check on the progress of the couple. According to Andersen, by the time the security manager called to say that Dodi and Diana were having dinner in the Imperial Suite, "Paul had already shaved and dressed and was headed out the door. In his pocket were his credit cards, his keys, a Casio digital calculator, his Ritz and Justice Ministry photo IDs, and an inexplicably large amount of cash...roughly $2,280.00. Paul had not been summoned back to the hotel; the decision to return to work...was entirely his." Does that not sound like a man who has been paid for a "job" and is headed *out* of the country? Perhaps additional funds had already been deposited in a Swiss bank account.

There were a number of partially filled liquor bottles in Paul's apartment. What does that prove? Nobody knows how full the bottles were earlier, or how long they had been there. We know how much alcohol was in his blood after the accident, but we don't really know how it or the large amount of carbon monoxide got there. He certainly didn't drink the carbon monoxide. Or maybe he needed a lot of "liquid courage" for the job he had to do. (His alcohol blood level was equal to about three glasses of wine.) Some witnesses claim he appeared to be drunk, but Rees-Jones, who was there and whose job it was to notice such things, stated unequivocally, "There was absolutely nothing untoward about his behavior." Certainly in the security camera clips shown on television he appeared to be functioning perfectly well. Long time friends refuted the idea that he was an alcoholic, with such statements as, "was not an alcoholic," "never lost control," "simply does not take unnecessary chances," "prudent, prudent, prudent." He was also described by friends as "intensely secretive"—he "compartmentalized" his relationships. That is what secret service agents have to do. He was said to be suffering from depression, but that is not what Andersen describes on that fatal evening. He was "grinning broadly," "uncharacteristically exuberant." A photographer reports that, "Paul was looking happy and excited." Clearly something big was in the air. Henri Paul had an assignment that night of August 31. It was to get the Princess and her companion in the Pont de l'Alma tunnel. (There was a shorter route to their destination.) Apparently he did not really know what was to happen—or perhaps the original plan misfired. One theory is that the plan was to kidnap Dodi and "scare him off;" it was never intended that Diana be killed. Maybe. But it was Diana who was a threat to the monarchy, not Dodi. She was becoming more powerful, and—through Prime Minister Tony Blair—her influence was spreading internationally.

What about the doctor who supposedly gave Diana first aid, then left not knowing who she was? Wouldn't he have been just a little bit curious about a beautiful blond woman in a luxury limousine? Are they so common in Paris? Wouldn't he have wondered about the mass of paparazzi swarming around the car? He stated that they did not interfere with his work. What work? He raised her head a little and gave her some oxygen—then left. (Yet other witnesses said they did interfere. Why would he say differently?)

Why would an emergency physician have a medical bag containing only one item (oxygen)? Who knows what really happened during those first few minutes with Diana—and Henri Paul? He was off-duty, but if he had a medical bag with him, why would it only contain oxygen?

I believe that Diana was killed—murdered—assassinated by the British Intelligence Service—or some group—because it was feared that she was a danger to the monarchy, and that Henri Paul was an agent. The driver of the white Fiat Uno was another one. There would have been others—perhaps posing as paparazzi, or hotel helpers, even rescue workers. She had to go. Did the decision come from the Prime Minister? From the Queen? Certainly not from the Prime Minister; they were a team. And not from the Queen either, although she might have said something like, "She has got to be stopped," never meaning that she should be killed. More likely it was one of those situations in which the "Establishment" knew what was best for the country, or perhaps someone high up in the Secret Service. Some of the MI6 people could be very unstable, as the Countess of Romanones makes clear. Spying is a very stressful occupation. Remember it is the Establishment that wants to maintain the status quo. Their life style depends on it. We may never know the truth. It is really irrelevant. It does not matter whether Diana was the victim of a carefully planned assassination, or simply of an impaired driver and bad luck. Either way she was still a martyr; the lamb to the slaughter. Her megastar status as future Queen of England combined with her subsequent lack of protection proved a deadly combination. Had Charles been a faithful husband, even a semi-faithful husband, (or if Diana had been the kind of person who was only interested in position and "appearances"), she would not have been in a Paris tunnel with Dodi Fayed. Completely apart from her being used to provide an heir to the throne of England, it required her death—and the public response to it—to wake up the monarchy, to force the royals to finally face the fact that unless the monarchy is relevant in today's egalitarian society, it is redundant, unnecessary, and too expensive.

Harold Brooks-Baker, managing director of Burke's Peerage, the ultimate who's who of royalty and aristocracy, and an ardent monarchist, probably said it best.

"They found a modern woman to be the mother of Charles's children and when they couldn't handle her, they kicked her out. They finally succeeded and today they stand guilty. Here was a victim of the monarchy. *Diana died a martyr.* We can only hope her death brings about another kind of palace rebellion. The House of Windsor is in desperate need of a major overhaul, and if it doesn't get one soon, I fear for the very existence of the monarchy in Briton." Perhaps Diana saved it.

Diana kept two sets of diaries, one of her official appointments and one of her private activities—more like a journal. According to Andrew Morton all royal members keep such a diary, which, at the end of the year, is bound and stored for posterity in the Tower of London to be opened in a hundred years. It would be interesting—and perhaps enlightening—to see if Diana's diaries are still in place and, if so, what information they contain which might be relevant.

For all her glamour, fame, and wealth, Diana was a tragic figure. An unwanted baby (her parents were desperate for a boy—they already had two girls), her childhood was shattered by the acrimonious divorce of her parents, her adolescence unsettled by her father's remarriage. She entered young into a marriage she hoped would bring her happiness and security. It brought neither. She struggled through fifteen years of hypocrisy and unfulfillment, finally creating a constitutional crisis in her urgent need to find personal fulfillment; to survive. Just as she was beginning to build a real life and make a real contribution to worldwide suffering, her life was unceremoniously snuffed out. Lonely in life, Diana died alone—no husband or lover, not her sons, not a friend or family member was with her during her long dying or for many hours later. Prince Charles, forty-eight year old future King of England, after considerable "discussion," finally gained the reluctant permission of his mother, the Queen of England, to accompany Diana's sisters to Paris to claim the body of the mother of his children and escort it back to London. It would not be appropriate, the Queen insisted.

While Diana could—and did—win battles, she could never win the war. As Lady Colin Campbell pointed out, ultimately she was not more powerful that the monarchy. Except by dying. In death she can do no wrong, make no mistakes. She will be forever young, beautiful and radiant. Intentionally or not, Diana was truly sacrificed to save the monarchy. She did far more than provide the heir to continue the House of Windsor. She brought the monarchy kicking and screaming into the 21st century. By her death—and the world reaction to it—the Queen at last understood the changing nature of the times and of the monarchy—that "modernizing" the monarchy requires much more than putting the royal menus on computers. It requires developing a relevant role in today's very complex society. The Queen understands and is already moving in that direction. Whether or not Charles understands remains to be seen—and appears doubtful at the moment. Diana was far more than a fashion icon. History will show that HRH Diana, The Princess of Wales, saved the monarchy, at least for the present, and in the process changed the course of British history.

Diana was not a classic beauty. Like the Duchess of Windsor, her nose was a bit too large and her chin too prominent, and her hands were quite large. (In some pictures her hands look startlingly like those of Ann Boleyn, the ill-fated wife of Henry VIII.) Both had the figure of a model, although Diana herself considered her waist a bit thick. Yet, also like the Duchess, it all went together beautifully. She had an innate sense of style. Her smile brightened like the sun and her amazing blue eyes could mesmerize or comfort as the occasion demanded. Although terribly human, there was something magical about her. The worldwide grief and mourning over the death of a princess most of us never met seems to be symbolic of something far greater. Diana, Princess of Wales, consciously or unconsciously represented fairy tales and dreams and "happily ever after," Prince Charming, King Arthur and the Knights of the Round Table—a forgotten but integral part of our psyche. She was also a torchbearer for all women trapped in unhappy marriages, all women who felt "not quite good enough." She proved that you can get out—but the cost for her was very high, for her and for us. With her death, we have been forced to recognize that fairy tales are just that—and it is overwhelmingly sad and frightening.

In many ways Diana's situation was not unlike that of Anne Boleyn, the ill-fated wife of Henry VIII. A big difference was that Diana had the full support of the people; the people despised "Nan Bullen," the commoner that (they felt) was the cause of the downfall of the Good Queen Katherine. Still, both were caught up in powerful political storms. Anne was in love with and planning to marry Henry Percy, heir to The Earl of Northampton. Once the King noticed her, her life was no longer her own. With no choice, she decided to go for broke.

She would be Queen, not a mistress to be discarded as used goods as her sister had been. Yet in both instances, it was all about an heir. Henry was desperate for a son—and not sure who to blame. Was it his fault? He couldn't handle that—it must be someone else's; his marriage must be cursed. He had much of the sensibility and emotionality that Charles has (he wrote poems and loved music), but Charles is not the leader, the politician, the "golden god" that Henry was.

Still, in both cases, the new Queen-in-waiting represented a new age. In the 16th century England was changing from Medieval to Renaissance; in the 20th century England was changing from Victorian to Modern. In both cases, there were new interests, far-reaching changes in society and politics. It was—in both cases—a time of out with the old and in with the new. In both instances, the women had no control over the political hurricane they were caught up in. Both had few resources other than their own wits. Both ended up dead at a young age.

Was Diana a genuine threat? Yes. She very well might have been. She personally would never have done anything to harm the British Establishment or the Monarchy. After all, as she herself said in her BBC Panorama Interview, why would she destroy her sons' futures? Still, others might have used her. Her very fame, popularity and naiveté made her a target for the serious political factions, unscrupulous or not. The Palace only had minimal control once she was "no longer a royal." As with Elizabeth Tudor to Queen Mary; and Mary, Queen of Scots, to Elizabeth I, others would have attempted to use her to further their own ambitions. All governments at all times take severe action against serious threats, real or perceived. Perhaps it really was for the good of England. Perhaps, once again, it must be done.

Diana was truly the lamb to the slaughter. If she had not died in that terrible car crash in the early morning hours of August 31, 1997, there would surely have been another accident. Empress Theodora once said, "For a king, death is better than dethronement and exile." Perhaps the same is true for a princess—however adored.

Penny Thornton, Astrologer to the Princess, said that when Diana first approached her she said, "I just wanted to know if there was light at the end of the tunnel." No, Diana, for you there was no light at the end of the Alma tunnel.

The saddest fact of all…she is still being used to generate revenue.

Nevertheless, Diana won. The British Monarchy will never be the same. Her son will be a King like no other—royal, but with the human touch; traditional in ritual but modern in function. Her son will show the world what a modern King can do for his country—and those of us still around will see the reflection of Diana in his every action. So, yes, Diana, there *is* light at the end of the tunnel—a shining star.

APPENDIX A

CAST OF CHARACTERS

Charles, Prince of Wales	Eldest son of Queen Elizabeth and Prince Philip; heir to the throne of England
Diana, Princess of Wales	Former wife of Charles, mother of Princes William (heir to the throne) and Prince Henry ("Harry"); nee Lady Diana Spencer
Queen Elizabeth II	Queen of the British Commonwealth; formerly Princess Elizabeth, daughter of King George VI and Queen Elizabeth; married to Philip, Duke of Edinburgh; mother of Princes Charles, Andrew, Edward, and Princess Anne, the Princess Royal.
Prince Philip, Duke of Edinburgh	The Queen's husband; formerly Prince Philip of Greece; also in line for the Danish throne.
King George VI	"Bertie," Prince Albert of Windsor, Duke of York, father of the Queen and Princess Margaret; second son of George V.
Queen Elizabeth, the Queen Mother	Lady Elizabeth Bowes-Lyon, Duchess of York, consort of King George VI and mother of the Queen and the Princess Margaret.
Duke of Windsor	David, Prince of Wales; Edward of Wales; Edward of Norfolk and Wales: King Edward VIII; Prince Edward; (first and only) Duke of Windsor, elder brother of King George VI.
Princess Margaret	Only sister of the Queen. Forbidden by the Queen to marry the man she loved, Group Captain Peter Townsend, she later married Antony Armstrong-Jones. She is the mother of Lady Sarah Armstrong-Jones and Viscount Linley.

Princess Anne, the Princess Royal	Only daughter of the Queen, mother of Peter and Zara.
8th Earl Spencer	Father of Diana
Frances Shand-Kydd	Mother of Diana
Lady Sarah Spencer	Older sister of Diana, at one time Charles's girlfriend. She suffered from anorexia. She is married to Neal McCorquodale.
Lady Jane Spencer	Sister of Diana; married to Robert Fellowes, Private Secretary to the Queen.
Charles Spencer	Diana's only brother; now 9th Earl Spencer.
Ruth, Lady Fermoy	Diana's grandmother, lady-in-waiting to the Queen Mother.
Sarah Ferguson	Diana's friend; married and divorced Andrew, Duke of York (brother of Prince Charles). Two daughters, Princesses Eugenie and Beatrice
Major Ronald Ferguson	Sarah's father; Prince Charles's polo manager.
Susan Barrantes	Mother of Sarah, Duchess of York ("Fergie").
Camilla Parker-Bowles	Ex-wife of Col. Andrew Parker-Bowles; Mistress to Prince Charles

APPENDIX B

FOOD IN WARTIME ENGLAND

In the United States, during World War II, every man, woman, and child was issued a food ration book. Sugar, coffee, and canned goods were rationed and could only be purchased with coupons. Sugar and coffee, of course, were imported and had to be rationed to assure that everyone had a fair share. Rationing of canned goods was primarily to prevent hoarding and, again, make sure everyone had a fair share. The Black Market was a problem as it always is in times like this. While all our efforts were going into the war effort, we had to feed this vast army we were sending all around the world. Fortunately, we still had a lot of rural areas and small communities where people could continue to produce food. Everyone, wherever they lived, was encouraged to grow "Victory gardens"—little plots of vegetables in our yards or where ever we had space. However, there was never a real shortage of food in the United States—just not always a complete choice.

England was a whole different story. An island nation, a small landmass, most of her food had to be imported. However, not only were all the ships, equipment and personnel tied up in the war effort, by 1944 German U-boats were sinking everything in the North Atlantic. Tons and tons of fighting equipment *and food* were at the bottom of the ocean. Hardly a transport ship could get through. Even before we officially entered the war, through the Lend Lease program, the United States was shipping both military equipment and food to Britain and

Russia. In Britain, there was a very real shortage of food—except for the royals and the very rich, who had their own sources of beef, venison, trout, salmon, strawberries, cream, etc. Yet even the royals lacked wheat flour, sugar, tropical fruits and many other items. The British Government made a real effort to help the people make the most of the food they had. They succeeded beautifully. Britons have never been healthier, before or since. They used very little meat and sugar. Saccharine was used as a substitute for sugar in both the US and in Britain. They used a lot of oatmeal since wheat had to be imported. They used "free" foods (dandelion greens, nuts, berries, etc) much as we did here in the United States during the Great Depression. They grew Victory gardens (as we did); everyone worked together and shared what they had. They even shared ovens in order to save fuel. The actual amount of food they lived on was amazing. Obesity was not a problem There was a tremendous advertising effort to remind people that they were contributing to the war effort by eating the healthful meals that could be prepared with only the foods available.

We were just beginning to learn about vitamins, both in the US and in England. (We still didn't know about cholesterol—but that was not a problem during the Depression or during the war.) The British Government, through its Ministry of Food, hired people similar to our Extension Agents, whose job was to develop healthy recipes and tips for making the most of what little food was available. They then distributed this information through newspapers, pamphlets and radio.

For a week, an adult would have something like 1 lb. of meat, plus 4 oz. ham and bacon; 2 oz. butter, 4 oz. margarine (it still wasn't colored), and up to ½ lb. cheese if it was available. Each person was allowed 3 pts. milk per week, plus powdered skim milk (I think it was enough to make 1 gal. per month); 1 "shell" egg (a real, whole egg) per week plus a packet of powdered egg each four weeks. There were also coupons for 2 oz. tea and ½ lb. sugar. (In the US extra sugar was allowed for canning. I don't think there *was* extra sugar in Britain.)

There was sometimes additional meat, fish, dried fruit or beans for which you could spend your "extra points." Babies, expectant and nursing mothers received concentrated orange juice, cod liver oil (none of us had yet learned to add vitamin D to milk), and priority milk from Welfare Clinics (similar to today's Well Baby Clinics).

Oatmeal was used in place of flour when possible and there were recipes for oatmeal pastry, oatmeal biscuits, oatmeal pancakes, etc. It was even used to thicken soups, stews and puddings as in this recipe for **Vegetable Soup.**

Fry 2 oz. oatmeal in 1 oz margarine. Blend with a little of 2 pints of water, then add the rest of the water and bring to a boil. Add 3 potatoes, 4 carrots, 1/2 small swede, 1 leek if you have it, sliced or cut into cubes. Cook for 1 hour. Just before serving add pepper and salt and some chopped parsley. Serves 4. (A swede is a kind of turnip.)

The British, surrounded by water, have always eaten a lot of fish. Some fish was still available, especially Fresh Salted Cod from Iceland (it must be soaked in fresh water for 24 to 48 hours, but this was usually done by the fishmonger before purchase), so there were many recipes for preparing fish. Still, the actual size of the serving was small by today's standards. A typical recipe might be the following:

Fish Potato Pie.

1 ½ lb. fresh-salted cod, freshened

2 cups fish stock and milk

2 Tbs. drippings or fat

1 Tbs. flour

1 ½ tsp. lemon substitute, if available

Salt and pepper

Parsley

Hot mashed potatoes

Cube fish, removing skin and bones. Put into a pan, cover with boiling water and simmer till fish is just tender. Drain, measure liquid and add milk to make 2 cups. Melt drippings in ovenproof pan, add flour and seasonings, stir, add liquid. Cook till thick and add fish. Cover with mashed potatoes and bake in hot oven until browned, about 15 minutes.

Ovens did not yet have thermostats and recipes simply stated, Hot, Moderate, etc. Also, measurements were not usually standardized. Most people still used actual teaspoons or "tablespoons," which varied from kitchen to kitchen. In England and in many parts of the US, there was still the fishmonger, the butcher, the greengrocer, etc., rather than today's "supermarket."

This recipe illustrates the various pastry recipes, as well as imaginative use of whatever food was available. Apricots were scarce and expensive, but carrots could be grown in the Victory gardens.

Mock Apricot Flan

Line a large 9-inch pie plate or flan dish with shortcrust pastry or oatmeal pastry or potato pastry. Bake in a hot oven for 20 to 25 minutes until firm and golden.

Meanwhile grate 1 lb. young carrots. Put in saucepan with a few drops of almond essence, 4 Tbsp. plum jelly and only about 4 Tbsp. water. Cook gently until a thick pulp. Spread into the cooked pastry. Spread a little more plum jam if this can be spared.

(The carrots are said to really taste a little like apricots.)

Of course, everyone was urged "not to waste," but there were also specific suggestions. Stale bread or breadcrumbs could be used to stretch meat dishes, in a "padded" pudding, as topping for a baked dish (such as scalloped potatoes). It could be toasted and used for breakfast cereal or for coating foods before frying or baking.

"Fat" should not be wasted—not only bacon fat (which could be used for seasoning or for frying), but cooks were encouraged to skim fat from stews or soups and save it to use in place of shortening. Many recipes called for a "butter paper" to be laid on top of the food before baking—assuming that at least a little of the butter was still sticking to the paper (and would not be wasted).

Fresh vegetable scraps were made into "vegetable broth" to be used as a base for soups and other recipes. Fish trimmings were to be made into fish broth.

Britons were urged to eat potatoes (cooked in the skin to conserve vitamins and minerals) every day (and eat less bread—not because it was less healthy, but because the wheat had to be imported and was very scarce). They should have at least one cooked and one uncooked vegetable everyday, with carrots being included several times a week.

Directions for preserving food for winter were also provided. There were, as yet, no home freezers, but food could be dried, pickled, "bottled" (canned), or made into jams or jellies (with limited amounts of both fruit and sugar).

It was a healthy diet, well ahead of its time. It is typical of the English who are a special breed of people. These people fought the superior German war machine with everything they had—and sometimes that was not much more than courage. They lived on a diet that most of us would think impossible today. They were bombed on an almost daily basis. (Four million buildings were destroyed.) The help they needed so desperately from the US kept ending up at the bottom of the ocean (and Americans were very reluctant to risk their own lives in this terrible war)—yet they never gave up, they never even considered defeat. The English people—the British people—are one of a kind.

Appendix C
NOTES

Chapter 1:

Henry VIII was desperate for an heir. The marriage of his parents, Henry Tudor and Elizabeth of York, had finally united the House of Lancaster (Henry's mother was a Lancaster) and the House of York, ending the thirty year Wars of the Roses and re-uniting England. Henry had the royal responsibility to continue the Tudor dynasty, only two generations old. His wife, Catherine of Aragon, was a good wife, but with only one living child, a daughter, Mary, she was past her childbearing years. Henry felt, (with good reason) that his only choice was to have his marriage declared invalid (he did not divorce her) and take a younger wife who could bear a healthy son.

1. Royal wedding cakes are quite different from the fluffy cakes decorated with flowers made of icing that we are familiar with. They are covered with a layer of creamy marzipan on which actual pictures are painted, and often feature fresh flowers.

2. This was the Cambridge Lover's Knot tiara, which Queen Mary had made by Garrard Jewelers in 1914, so named because it was a copy of one owned by her grandmother, Princess of Augusta of Hess and Duchess of Cambridge.

3. The phrase, "she made herself sick," is often used to describe Diana's illness. This tends to suggest that the gorging was something she chose to do (and therefore could choose not to do).

Nothing could be further from the truth. It would be more accurate to say that the food made her ill and she had to get rid of it, just as eating something toxic would make you sick and you would have to get rid of it. Bulimia is not about eating, or slimming: it is about feeling out of control and trying to regain some measure of control.

4. Many writers have said that Prince Charles said, "Whatever love is." He said, "Whatever *in* love is." There is a big difference—and, of course, he knew (as the world did not) that Camilla would be watching very carefully. (However, according to Diana, he did say, "Whatever love is," when he proposed and she was saying, "I love you so much.")

Chapter 2:

When the youngest son of King George V and Queen Mary was born mentally retarded and epileptic, this was still considered a shameful thing—something to be hidden. It was not unusual for such children to be kept "hidden," even in non-royal families. There was still a sense of such things being the result of the "sins of the fathers."

1. Althorp was built on 350 (now 1500) acres in the 1500's, during the Tudor period. The palatial residence is filled with a fabulous collection of paintings and other art.

2. Yet, shortly before Diana's death Diana's mother behaved in much the same way toward her own daughter when she gave an interview to *Hello!* Magazine, not taking Diana's side in the marital problems. Diana was said to be furious.

3. During the very correct courtship, under the careful supervision of chaperones, Diana was devastated when the media reported that she had spent several hours on two consecutive nights on the royal train (with Prince Charles). The Palace stepped in at this point and

demanded an apology. It was some time before someone realized that "the blond woman" who had been seen boarding the train was Camilla, not Diana. (Charles, who knew very well who the blond woman was, in New Delhi, spoke out on the "sensationalism" of the British media and the lack of morals in reporting.)

4. Most writers have the proposal taking place at a cozy dinner for two in the Prince's Buckingham Palace apartments. According to Diana, he proposed in the nursery of Windsor Castle. She does not mention dinner.

5. She would be the 9th Princess of Wales. To put this in perspective, Katherine of Aragon, the first wife of Henry VIII, was the 3rd Princess of Wales.

6. The wedding itself was organized by Edward Adeane, the Prince's Private Secretary, and by the Lord Chancellor.

7. Only much later did we learn that he spent his wedding eve night with Camilla. (See chpt. 3, #8)

Chapter 3:

Although a direct descendent of Queen Victoria, King George V was German. His name was Sax-Coburg-Gotha. Relations with Germany were breaking down as the build-up to World War I began. The English people were starting to hate everything German. The King (and his advisors) felt it wise for him to change his name. He chose the name of his favorite residence, Windsor—and thus the House of Windsor was born. Meanwhile, in Russia, the people were rebelling against the Czar (or Tsar). There was real danger. The Czar, cousin of the King, requested asylum in England. The King was sympathetic, but the Czar's wife was German and proud of it. The King's advisors convinced him he should refuse. The Czar and his family were subsequently executed.

1. Contrary to many reports, Charles was not the oldest heir to the throne at the time of his marriage. At forty-one, his great-uncle David, Prince of Wales (later Edward VIII) was.

2. Like Diana, the Queen, too, understood the danger of being "sent away" (like her favorite Uncle David) if you did not do your duty. As a child she, too, showed signs of obsessive-compulsive behavior, lining her horses up in rigid formation and getting up repeatedly during the night to check on them.

3. For those who might not know, Nazis were Adolph Hitler's German political party and were responsible for World War II, Germany's aggression and the persecution and near annihilation of the Jews in all of Europe. They were bitterly hated by both the British and the Americans and were blamed for the most devastating war of all time.

4. Formerly Battenberg, King George V required Lord Mounbatten's name to be Anglicized also.

5. The Queen does not need a passport or a driver's license. She can declare war or dissolve Parliament, among other things. She can never be charged with a crime, even if she murders her husband in front of witnesses. Yet her real "power" is simply in who she is.

6. The "red boxes" contain the official government papers which are delivered daily to the monarch wherever he or she happens to be. Many of the papers require the monarch's signature or other action. No one else has access to them. She could have shared then with Prince Philip, as Queen Victoria did with her husband, Prince Albert, but she chose not to.

7. She may want to be Queen now. She is trying hard to change her image and gain the acceptance of the people—and Charles is willingly paying the bill.

8. Camilla and another confidante, Kanga, Lady Tryon, are said to have made up a short list for Charles to choose from (women who would not interfere with their own relationship with the Prince)—and Diana's name headed the list. I don't quite understand how these two women—both "confidantes" of the Prince (a euphemism for mistresses) managed to have such a friendly relationship. Charles eventually chose Camilla and Kanga, I believe, committed suicide.

9. According to James Whittaker, Prince Charles's valet, Stephen Barry, said he could not believe Charles would take such a risk, "carrying on with Camilla right up to the final moments of the bachelorhood...But when he took her to bed in the very week of his wedding it seemed incredible. Certainly incredibly daring, if not incredibly stupid." This does sound incredible until you think about it. First of all, Charles has been seeing her all along—but he has promised to stop once he is married. (Camilla never promised.) Tomorrow he will be married. This is his last chance. He can't do without this woman. They just had the fantastic pre-wedding ball for all the royal guests. It lasted until the wee hours of the morning. Everyone is tired and hung over. More importantly, Diana, who has been living next door, has been sent to the Queen Mother's house to rest and get ready for the big day. He may never have another chance (or so he believes at the moment).

Chapter 4:

When Henry VIII's daughter Mary ascended the throne, she was aware that Elizabeth, her younger half-sister (Anne Boleyn's daughter) was very popular among the people. Mary was determined to turn England back to its "true religion" and to the Pope. She believed fervently that this was her mission. She was saving souls. (She was also avenging her ill-treated mother, Queen Katherine.) Mary had almost been a mother to the orphaned Elizabeth at times, but she understood that her first loyalty was to England, and that others would use Elizabeth as a rallying point to overthrow her and put Elizabeth on the throne. (Elizabeth was, of course, Protestant.) She was urged to have her executed, but she could not quite bring herself to do that. Instead, Elizabeth was imprisoned in the Tower. Even that was temporary—but long enough for Elizabeth to learn her lesson; she had learned to be very, very careful.

1. The Church of England did not recognize divorce. As King, David would be Supreme Govenor of the Church of England. It was unthinkable that his Queen could be a divorced woman. (At this time, divorced women were not even allowed in the royal presence—which created quite a dilemma when David brought Wallis to visit his brother and his wife, the Duke and Duchess of York.)

2. As it turned out, David, Prince of Wales, was also unsure about being King. On several occasions he had talked about not being King and had gone so far as to purchase a ranch in Canada, where he told friends he planned to live.

3. Not only was David (Duke of Windsor now) *not* invited to his niece's wedding; he was instructed to *deny* that he was not invited. He was invited to participate in Elizabeth's coronation, but without his wife. However, Margaret Biddle was giving a Coronation party in Paris and invited him to narrate. The United Press offered him "a fat fee" for the rights to the narration and he accepted. He did everything he was told, believing it would eventually allow his return to England.

4. These were royal jewels which the Duke of Windsor (as Prince of Wales and King Edward VIII) had given to his Wallis. More than fabulous jewels, they were bits of British history.

5. The lives of these two people with so much potential was an utter waste of royal make-believe. Both could (and would) have made major contribution to the war effort and to England, but they were not allowed to. There are no roles for an illegally exiled ex-king and his mistress-wife.

6. After Peter Townsend's exile, the Queen Mother denied that he ever held such a position.

7. The former Queen gave herself the title of Queen Elizabeth, the Queen Mother. No other dowager queen has retained her title of Queen.

8. Even in her nineties the Queen Mother continued to be powerful, keeping from the public certain documents from World War II that she feared would reflect badly on George VI, reading the riot act to Charles regarding his duty over pleasure, even calling in Andrew Parker-Bowles (Camilla's husband) and pressuring him not to divorce Camilla as it could cause "a constitutional crisis." After having her butler read her the story of Fergie's latest scandal, she picked up the phone and called the Queen. Fergie was history.

9. Fergie is slowly and carefully working her way back into a comfortable niche.

Chapter 5:

Mary, Queen of Scots, a lovely young dowager Queen, both of France and of Scotland, mother of a young son, was in danger of her life. She escaped to England, where she petitioned Queen Elizabeth for asylum. This presented a real dilemma for Elizabeth. Mary was a cousin; a sister monarch, yet Elizabeth knew that as long as Mary lived, her enemies would use her as a rallying point. (If she tended to forget, her advisors quickly reminded her.) They urged her to have Mary executed. She resisted until, finally, they brought her proof positive of a plan to dispose of her and put Catholic Mary on the throne. Elizabeth I had no choice but to sign the order for her execution.

1. I learned this word from Princess Diana.

2. She was also a bit of an exhibitionist. Her obsession with her body and her love-hate relationship with the media further demonstrated her almost pathological need for affirmation—"Look at me; tell me I'm okay." This was exacerbated by the fact that everybody *was* looking at her—all the time. It had to be exhausting—and was frequently misinterpreted.

3. The 23.6 carat brilliant cut rare pink diamond is the center of a jonquil-shaped flower with petals, stems and leaves of diamonds. The brooch is 4 ½" long and was worn in a formal portrait of the Queen and four-year old Princess Anne. The diamond was cut from a 54.5 carat stone given to the Queen as a wedding gift in 1947.

4. Of special interest to me was the way the Prince and Princess coordinated their outfits. Diana had two dressers and Charles had at least two valets. They must have worked in tandem. When Charles wore the uniform of Commander of the Royal Navy, Diana wore her chic Catherine Walker navy and white pinstripe suit with a white sailor hat. When Diana wore her pink silk solid and stripe dress, Charles wore a pink carnation boutonnière. Always they complemented one another.

Chapter 6:

David, Prince of Wales, had fallen in love with an American divorcee. When his father died and he became King Edward VIII, he was told that he had to choose between the woman and the throne. This might not have been entirely true. Apparently, David never questioned it. Wallis Simpson had him in thrall, just as Camilla has Charles in thrall today. He chose the woman—and probably would have whatever the consequences—but no one told him he would never again be allowed to even live in England.

1. Lest you doubt Diana's sincerity relating to her care and compassion for the ill and disabled, read the "Squidgy" tape. In a conversation she believes to be entirely private, she describes a visit to her old home, Park House, which is now a home for the disabled. She clearly demonstrates her care and concern for those less fortunate than herself.

2. By now, everyone has heard the comments on the Camillagate tapes, especially the more embarrassing parts. More important, however, are Charles's comments about the strike. At this time a very serious ambulance driver's strike is taking place. It is costing lives. The police and the army are attempting to provide temporary service. Camilla's husband, Andrew, is coordinating the effort, which is taking a lot of his time. Charles, the future King of England, is not worried about the strike and its effects; he is worried that it might end before he has a chance to see Camilla.

3. If $26,000,000.00 seems like a lot, compare it to settlements of movie stars and other celebrities.

4. "Life" turned out to be only months.

5. But we should not forget that it all started in England with the Magna Carta, and that our Congress is modeled after British Parliament.

6. According to A.N. Wilson (*The Rise and Fall of the House of Windsor*), "The Establishment had decided long before the 'abdication crisis' that they would get rid of the king…"

7. See Appendix B.

8. The strong symbolism of the Queen attempting to douse the flames of Windsor while her husband played in South America and her children were elsewhere was not lost on the Queen and her supporters.

9. Conceivably, Parliament could pass such an Act, or even do away with the Monarchy completely, without the Queen's permission, but this is *highly* unlikely.

Chapter 7:

Two young nephews—brothers—stood between Richard III and the throne. He thought that it would be better for England to have an adult King (himself). He simply had the two innocent boys smothered in their sleep. His reign was short-lived. The English people would not have it. The young Henry Tudor returned from safekeeping in France, met Richard III on the battlefield. Richard was defeated and Henry was crowned King of England. The Tudor dynasty had begun.

1. It has been reported that one of the Queen's first questions on learning of Diana's death was whether she was wearing jewelry. (She means royal jewelry.) She is said to have called the French Embassy and demanded their return. If true, I have some sense of where she was coming from. Nevertheless, it was unseemly. First of all, the Queen, for all her apparent composure must surely have been in shock like everybody else. Secondly, when the Duchess of Windsor died—also in Paris—even though the Duchess had agreed for her jewels to be returned from whence they came, the royals had a hard time getting them back. (They inadvertently ended up in the wrong hands.) The Queen was surely remembering this. To us they are fantastic jewels; to the Queen they are bits of history for which she is responsible

2. It has also been reported that the nurses at the hospital where Diana died placed the rosary in her hand. This seems unlikely.

They would not have had access to it. It was likely at her home in London. If she did travel with it, it would have been sent with her other things to London already. (Dodi's father had all their things packed up and shipped out quickly since he did not know what was happening.) It is said that she was clutching the rosary and pictures of her boys in her hands when she died. This seems highly unlikely. In an accident of this nature, it is hard to imagine her groping through her handbag to get these items even if she had them with her and had been able to. That is not the sort of thing a young woman typically takes on a date. She was barely conscious—and she was dying for a long time—almost four hours. One story is that her trusted butler brought with him the pictures of the boys that she always traveled with. Again, if she always traveled with them, how could he bring them from London? (Possibly he brought the rosary when he brought clothes for her to be dressed in before her family arrived.) Apparently the pictures and the rosary were placed in her hands sometime before she was buried.

3. Prince Andrew, Prince Edward and Viscount Linley also bowed. Princess Margaret and Princess Anne did not.

4. When grief is unbearable, it turns into anger, which is only slightly more bearable.

5. The Queen had the power to order a state funeral.

6. Use of a lead lined casket is also a royal tradition. The body of Henry VIII was "encased in lead;" his mother, Elizabeth of York, was buried in a lead lined casket.

7. It has been said that Philip was her severest critic. Not so. He could be blunt and harsh, but they understood each other and she had tremendous respect for him. He often supported and encouraged her—until Morton's book, *Her True Story* was published.

8. Queen Victoria died in 1901. It seems that her coffin would have been carried on a ceremonial gun carriage.

9. The song, "Candle in the Wind," was originally written for Marilyn Monroe, who also died tragically at the age of thirty-six.

10. Diana's funeral really was a royal funeral, although not a state affair. It had all the trappings of a royal funeral: Wellington Arch, Westminster Abbey, lead-lined casket, everything except the guests were "the people," rather than the kings and queens attending most royal funerals.

Chapter 8:

The vain, aged, lonely Virgin Queen Elizabeth imagined love with the young Earl of Essex, nephew to her real love, Robert (Robin) Dudley, Earl of Leicester. He had fawned and flattered, but finally he betrayed her. He raised an army against her. It was her power and throne that he wanted, not her love. Though it broke her heart, she had no choice but to sign the warrant for his execution.

1. It was later claimed that the Mercedes was not armoured. If not, why not?

2. Lady Tryon: "What I suggest is that people stop and think deeper about all these so-called revelations [tapes]. I believe that republican groups are trying to undermine the country and bring the monarchy down. I suggest the people and the press are being maneuvered by somebody to bring about the monarchy's destruction." Then, of course, there was Susan Barrantes, mother of Sarah, Duchess of York, who was killed in a bizarre car accident in South America.

3. The Queen ordered no radio or television at Balmoral. This was her way of trying to protect the boys from all the media exposure.

Reportedly, she did not even discuss their mother's death with the boys. I really doubt this. According to Christopher Andersen (*The Day Diana Died*) the Queen was asked if any changes should be made in the planned church service and the answer was, "No."

4. It was later reported that the owner of the limousine, Philippe Siegel, knew of "persistent and unexplained" problems with the brakes.

5. Someone supposedly came forth eventually with a story that his white Citroen AX was the mystery car. The car that left a bit of itself on the Mercedes was a white Fiat Uno.

6. There is a scenario under which this would be possible. When (or if) Charles becomes King, then William will likely become Prince of Wales. Should he then marry, his wife would be Princess of Wales and Diana would presumably have been the Dowager Princess of Wales, but there cannot be both a wife and a former wife with the title.

7. I saw a re-enactment of this on television, based on skid marks and other evidence. It was very convincing.

Further Notes:

Diana has said that her intuition told her that Charles will never be king—and I have a lot of faith in Diana's intuition. Charles is behaving more and more like his Great-uncle David, who abdicated because he felt he "could not rule without the help of the woman he loved."

It is assumed that William will be King. However, some of Britain's best kings have not been the first born, but the second son. Henry VIII was a second son; the Queen's father was a second son. Harry would be King Henry IX.

It was reported that Diana's mother was satisfied that Diana could not have survived such an injury. I have to disagree. I have read and re-

read the details. Unless I am missing something very important, she was not badly injured at all. Aside from some superficial cuts and bruises; some broken bones (reports vary—but apparently she had several broken ribs and a broken arm), her only real injury was a tear in the pulmonary vein that carries blood from the heart to the lungs. This is a rare injury, and a very serious one—one that can be repaired, but it must be repaired very quickly. Had this been done, there is a very good chance that she would still be smiling and laughing today. She bled to death because the injury was not attended to for almost two hours. Worse, she was being given CPR by the trauma team, which was only increasing the rate of blood loss. The medical team could see her blood pressure was falling steadily—a sure sign of internal bleeding—why didn't they rush her to a hospital?

APPENDIX D

BIBLIOGRAPHY

I have been learning about the royal family since the newsreels of the 1930's. There is no way that I can credit all my sources. They have come from radio, newsreels, television, magazines, newspapers and books, over half a century. Following are some of the more recent ones I have found useful.

Andersen, Christopher, *The Day Diana Died*, NY: St. Martin's Press, 1998.
Baskin, Richard, *Princess Diana, Her Life Story,* Lincolnwood, IL, Publications Int., Ltd., 1997.
Bryan, J. III and Murphy, Charles J.V., *The Windsor Story*, NY, Dell Pub., 1979.
Cassini, Oleg, *A Thousand Days of Magic*, NY: Rizzoli, 1995.
Diagnostic and, Statistical Manual, IV, American Psychiatric Association, Washington, D.C., 1994.
Edwards, Anne, *Royal Sisters*, NY, Jove Publishers, 1991.
Field, Leslie, *The Jewels of Queen Elizabeth*, NY: Harry N. Abrams, Inc., 1987.
Graham, Tim & Blanchard, Tamsin, *Dressing Diana*, Princeton: Welcome Rain, 1998.
--------------*The Royal Year, 1990*, Summit Books, NY: 1990.
Hall, Trevor, *Born to Be King*, NY: Greenwich House, 1982.
Higham, Charles and Mosely, Roy, *Elizabeth and Philip*, NY, Double Day, 1991.

Holden, Anthony, *Charles at Fifty,* N Y: Random House, 1998.

----------------*A Princely Marriage*, NY: Bantam Press, 1991.

Levenson, David and Hall, Trevor, *The Story of Diana*, NY: Crescent, 1985

----------------*Charles and Diana's First Royal Tour*, NY: Crescent Books, 1983

----------------*Charles and Diana, Tour of North America*, NY: Greenwich: 1983.

----------------*Crown Jewels,*

Morton, Andrew, *and Buckingham Palace,* NY: Simon and Schuster, 1991.

--------------------*Diana's Diary,* NY: Simon and Schuster, 1990.

--------------------*Diana, Her New Life,* NY: Simon and Schuster, 1994.

--------------------*Diana, Her True Story,* NY: Simon and Schuster, 1992.

--------------------*In Her Own Words,* NY: Simon & Schuster, 1997.

Patten, Marguerite, *We'll Eat Again,* Reed International Books, 1985.

Spink, Kathryn, *Invitation to a Royal Wedding*, NY: Crescent, 1981.

Whitaker, James, *Diana v. Charles, the Royal Blood Feud,* NY: Penguin Books USA, Inc., 1993.

Wouk, Herman, *War and Remembrance,* NY, Pocket Books, *1993*.

York, Sarah, Duchess of, *My Story,* NY: Simon & Schuster, 1996.